Adidas Wilson

P.O. Box 1775

Antioch, Tn. 37115

siriusvisionstudios@gmail.com

www.adidaswilson.com

Orders by U.S. trade bookstores and wholesalers.

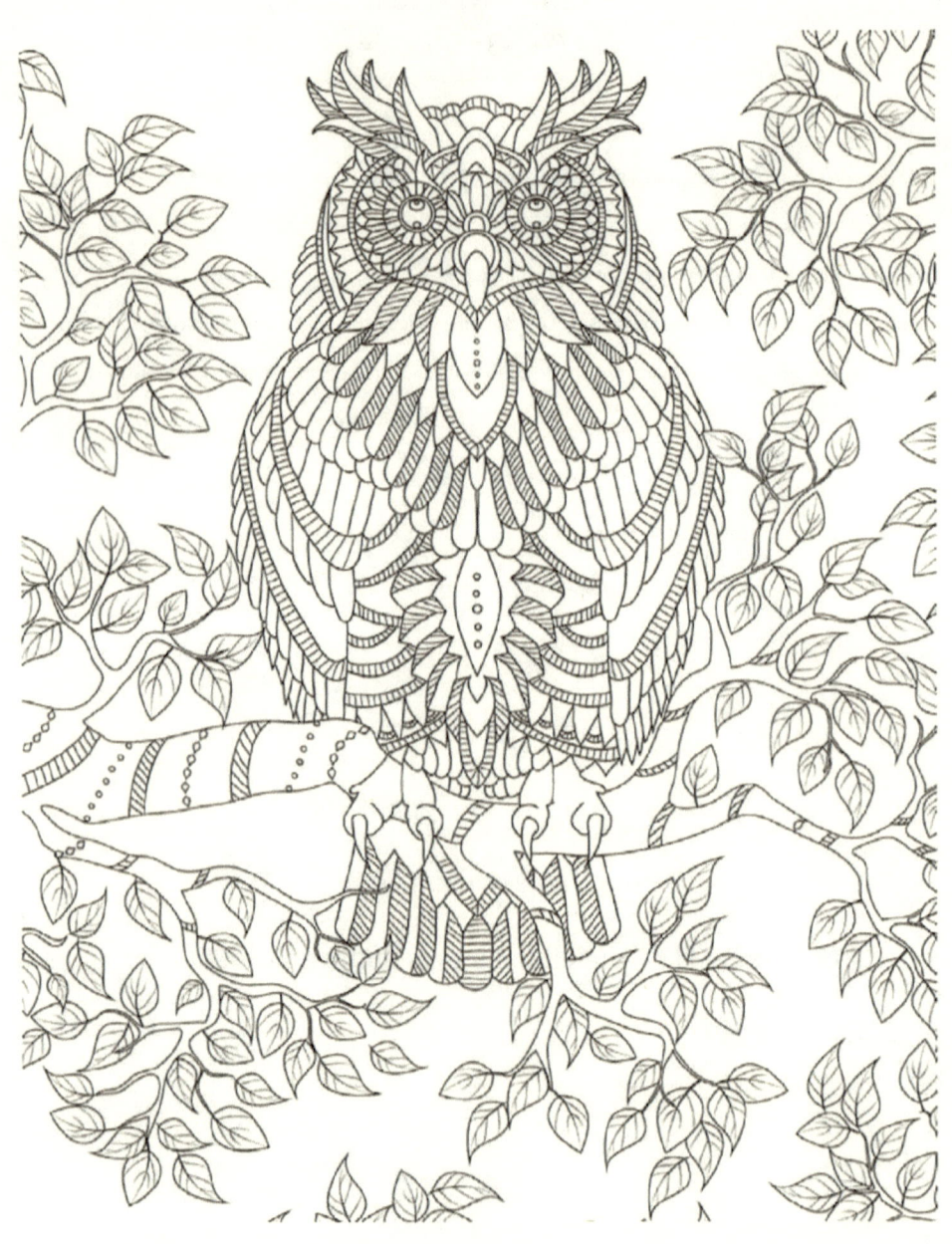

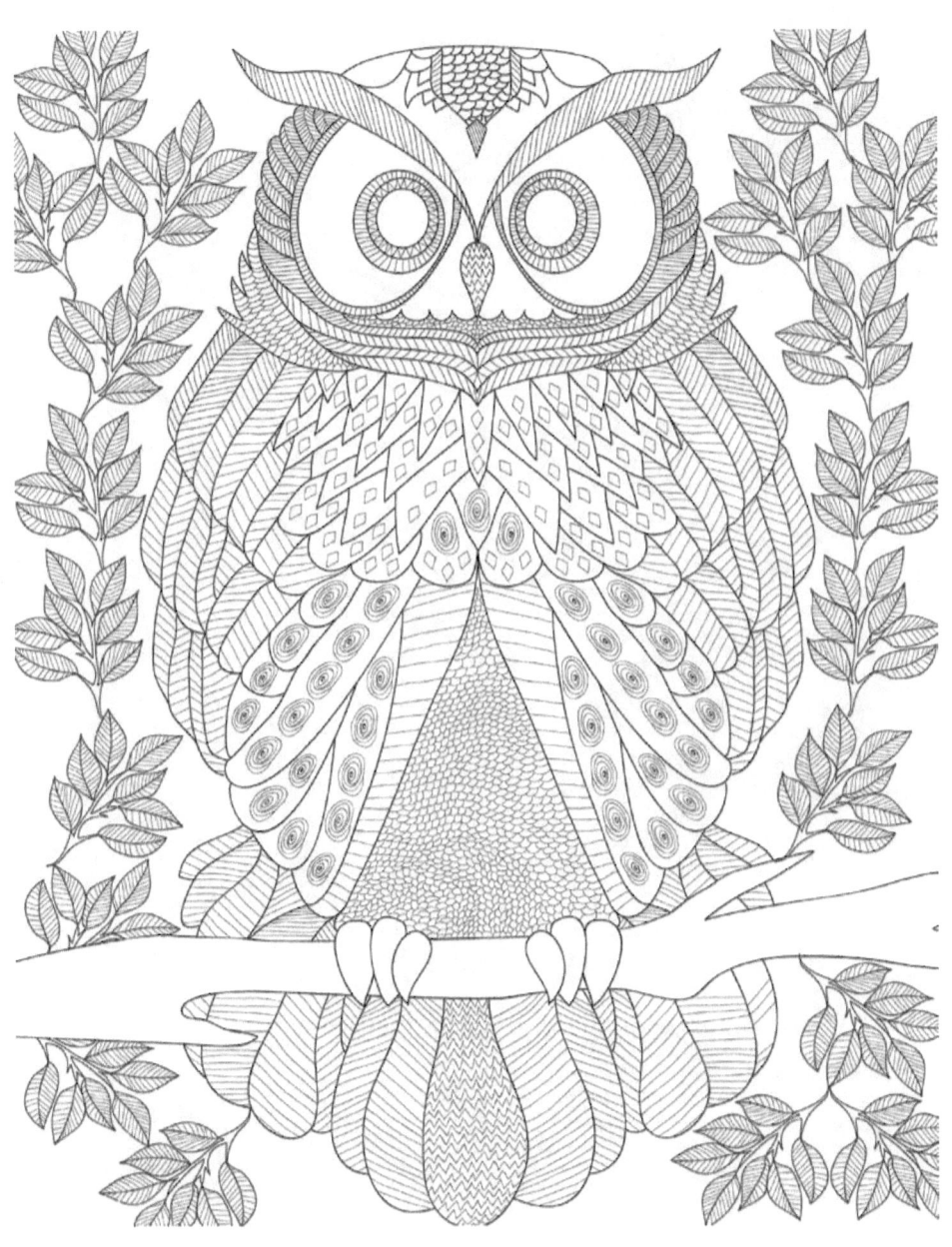

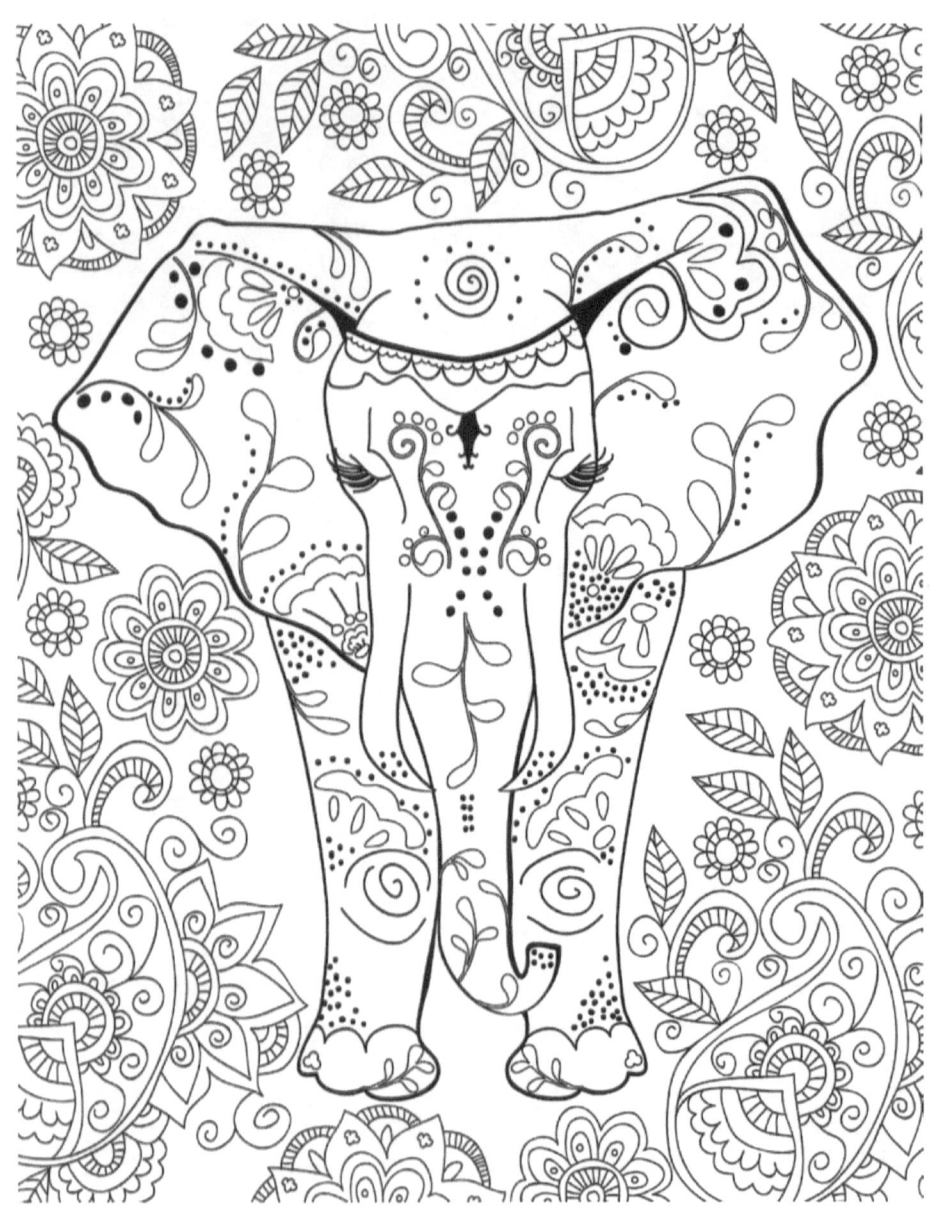

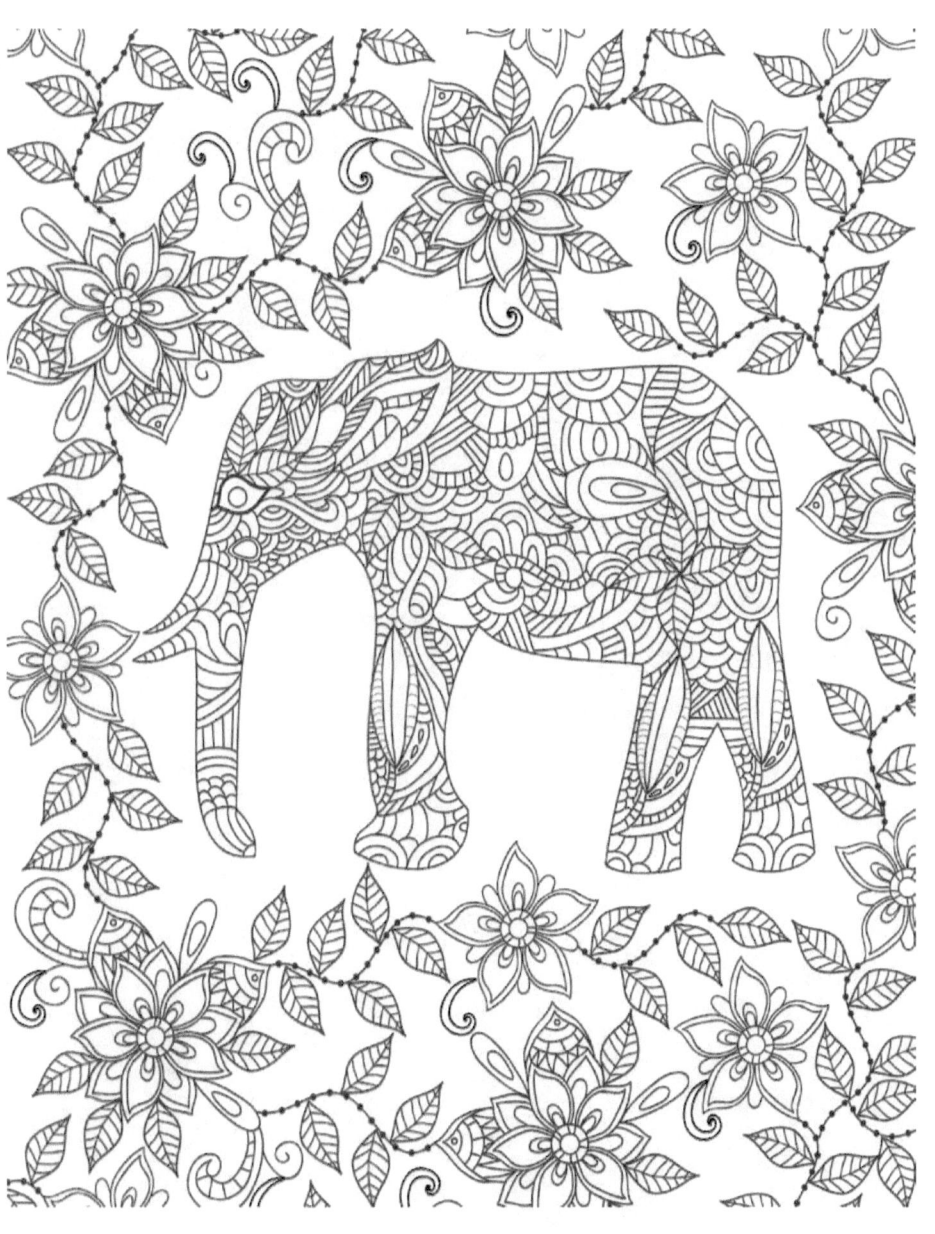

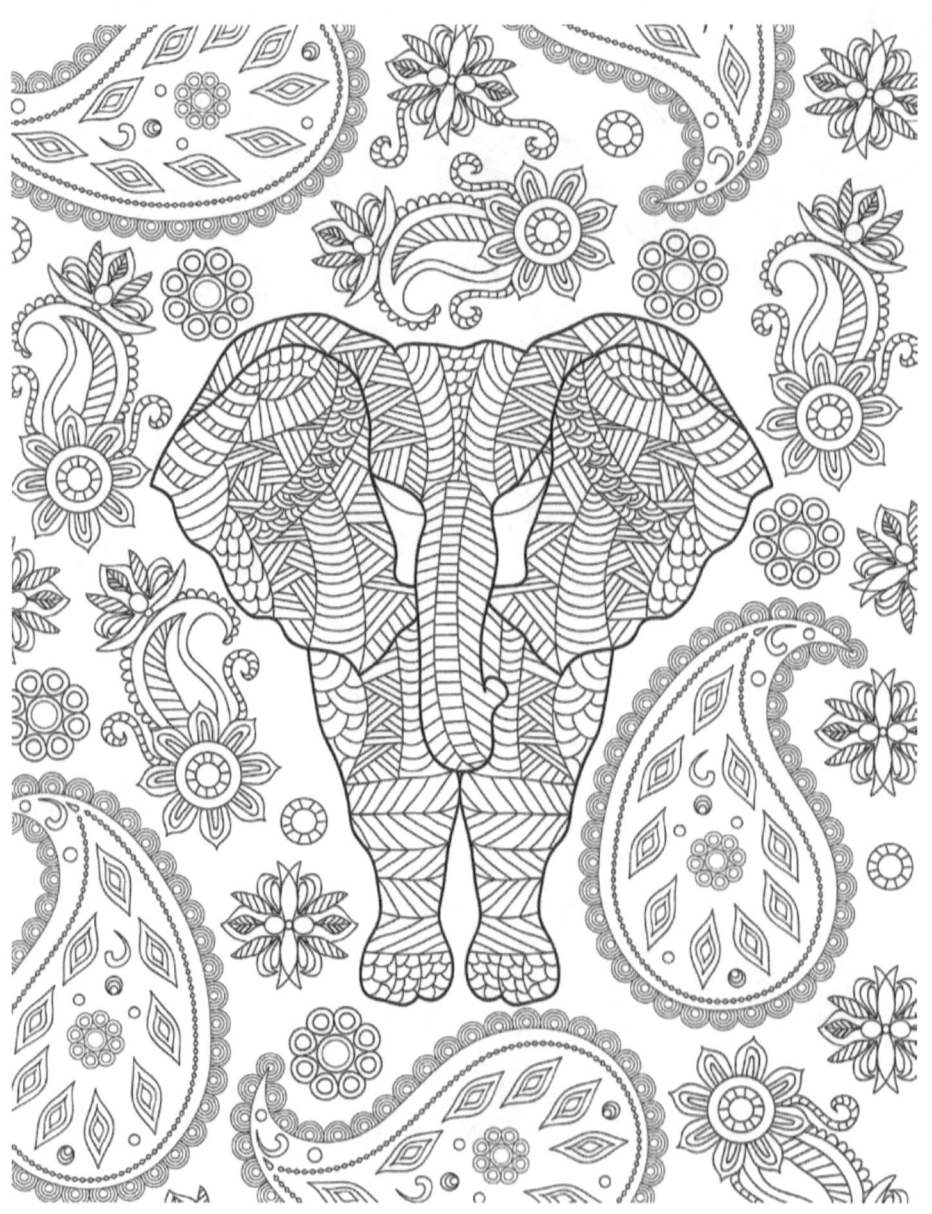

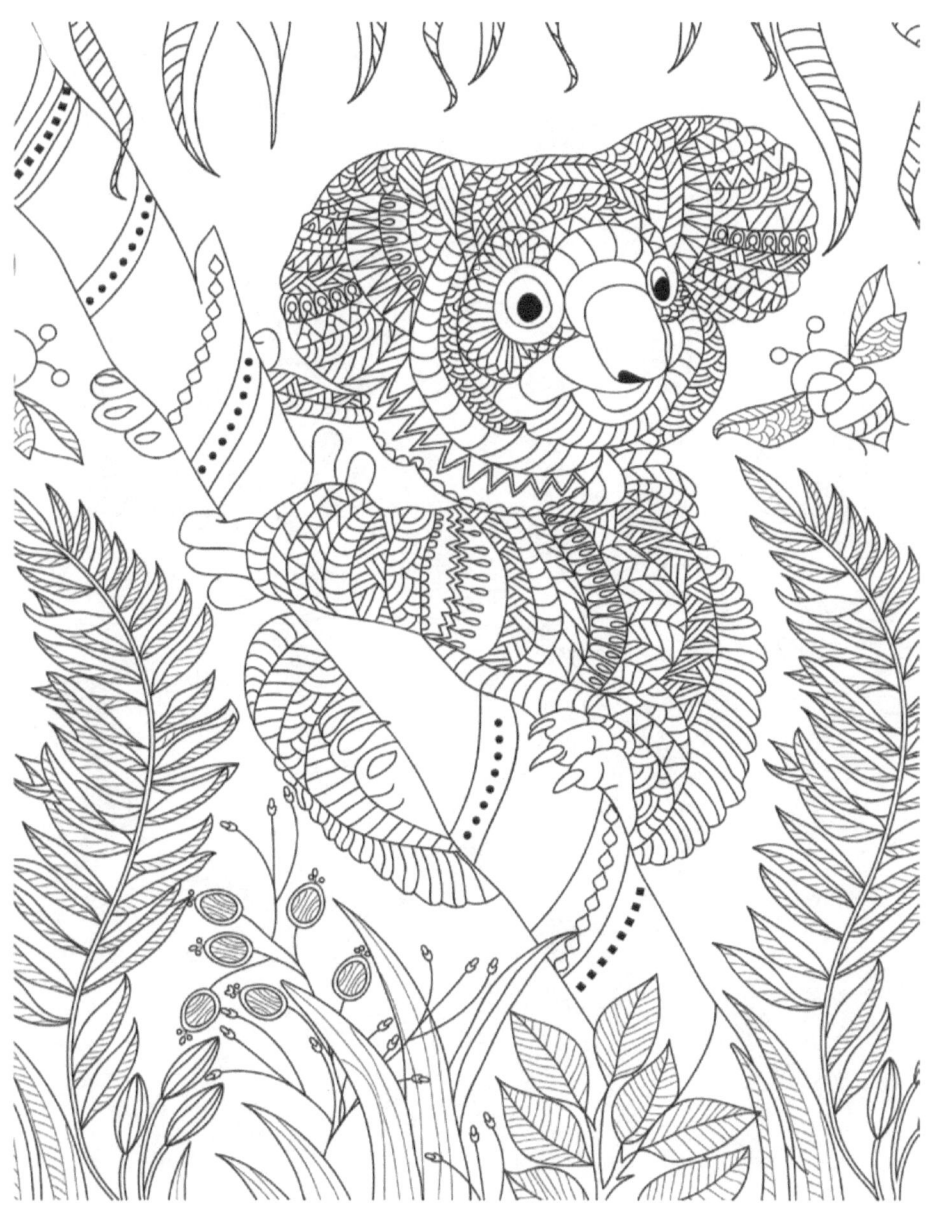

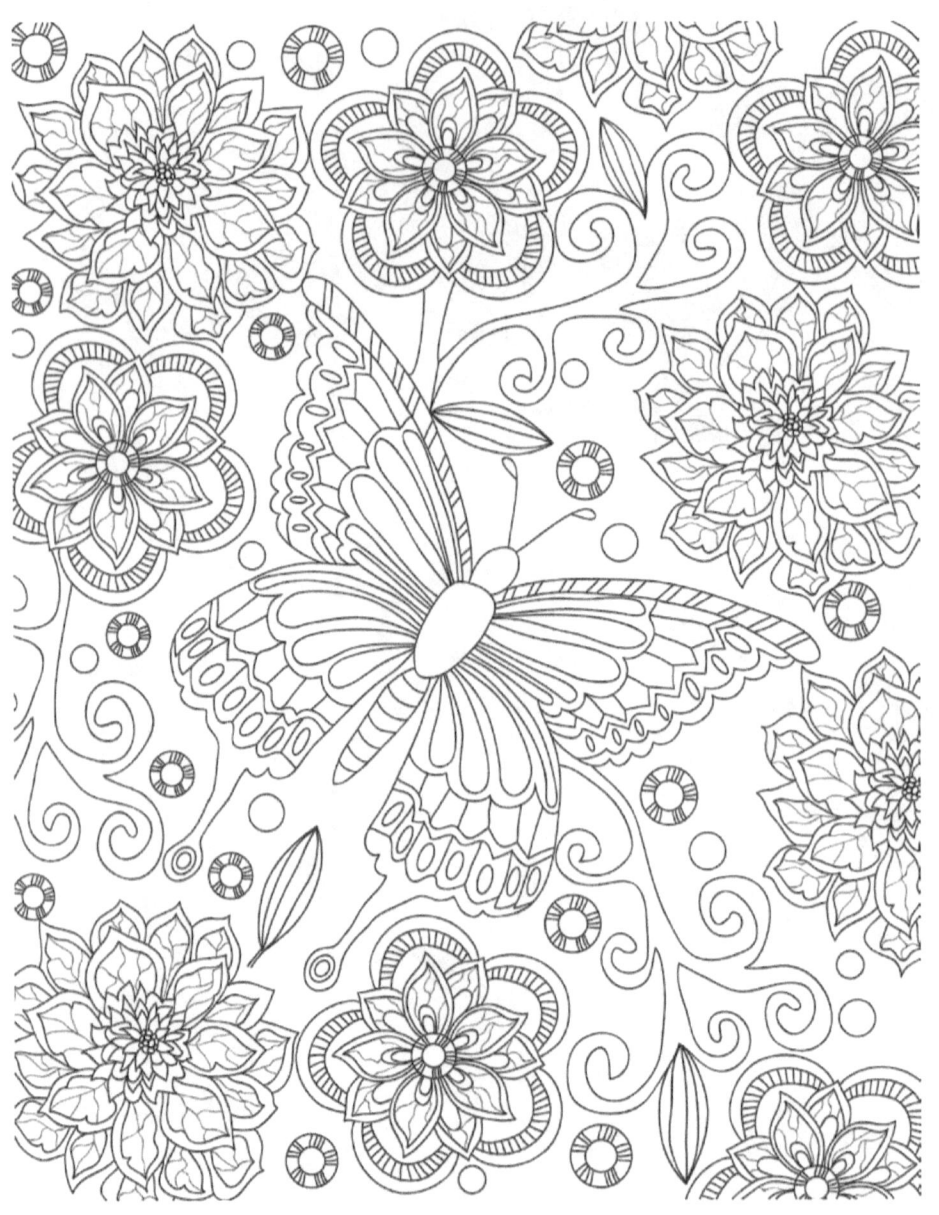

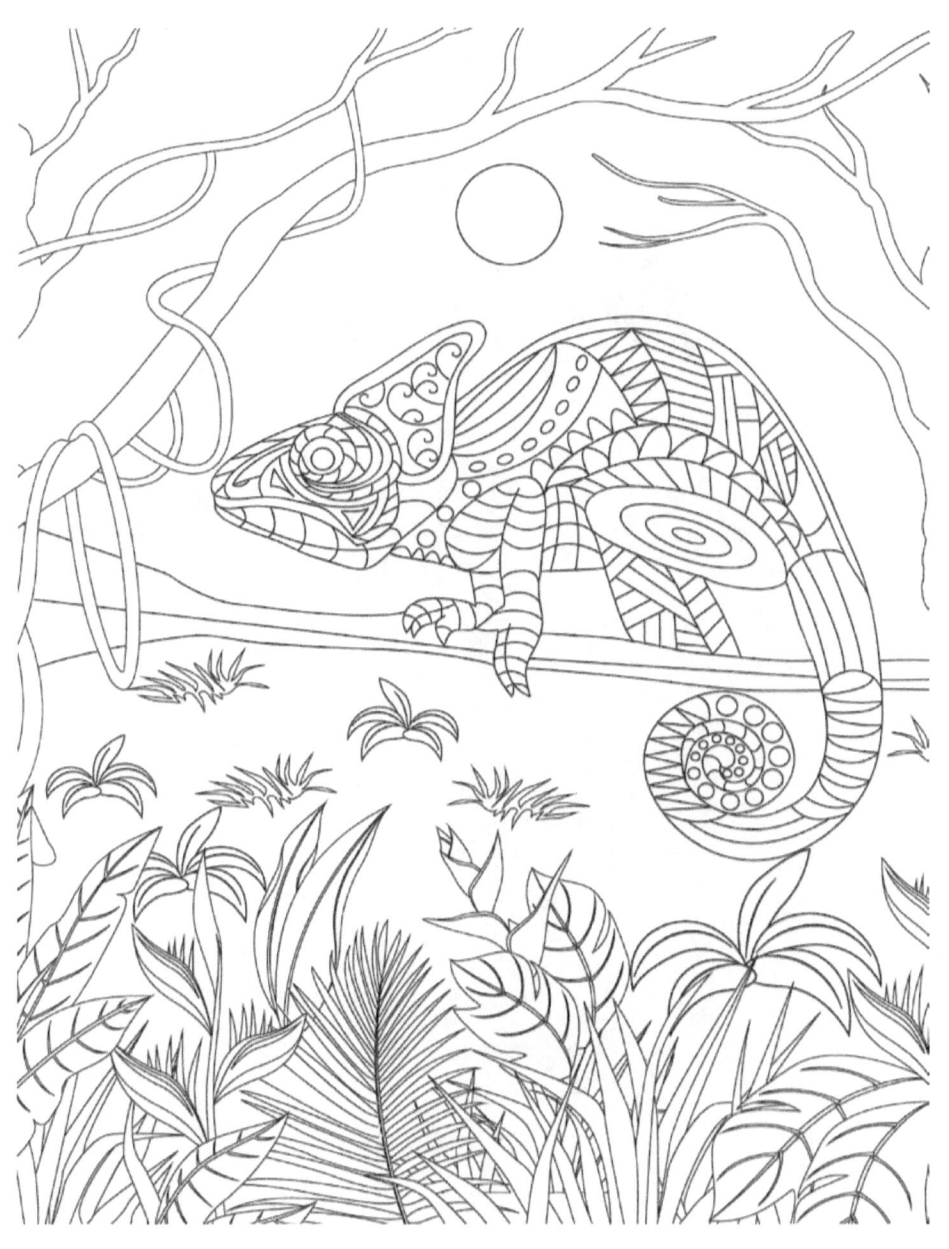

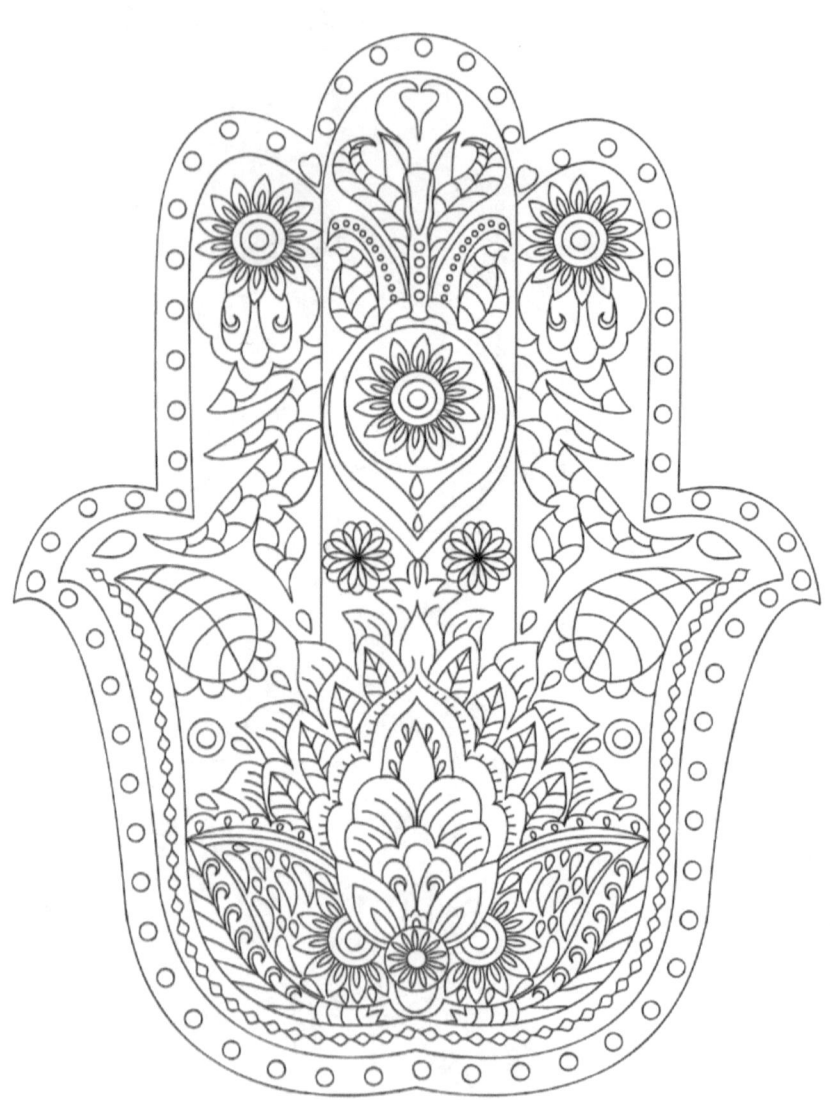

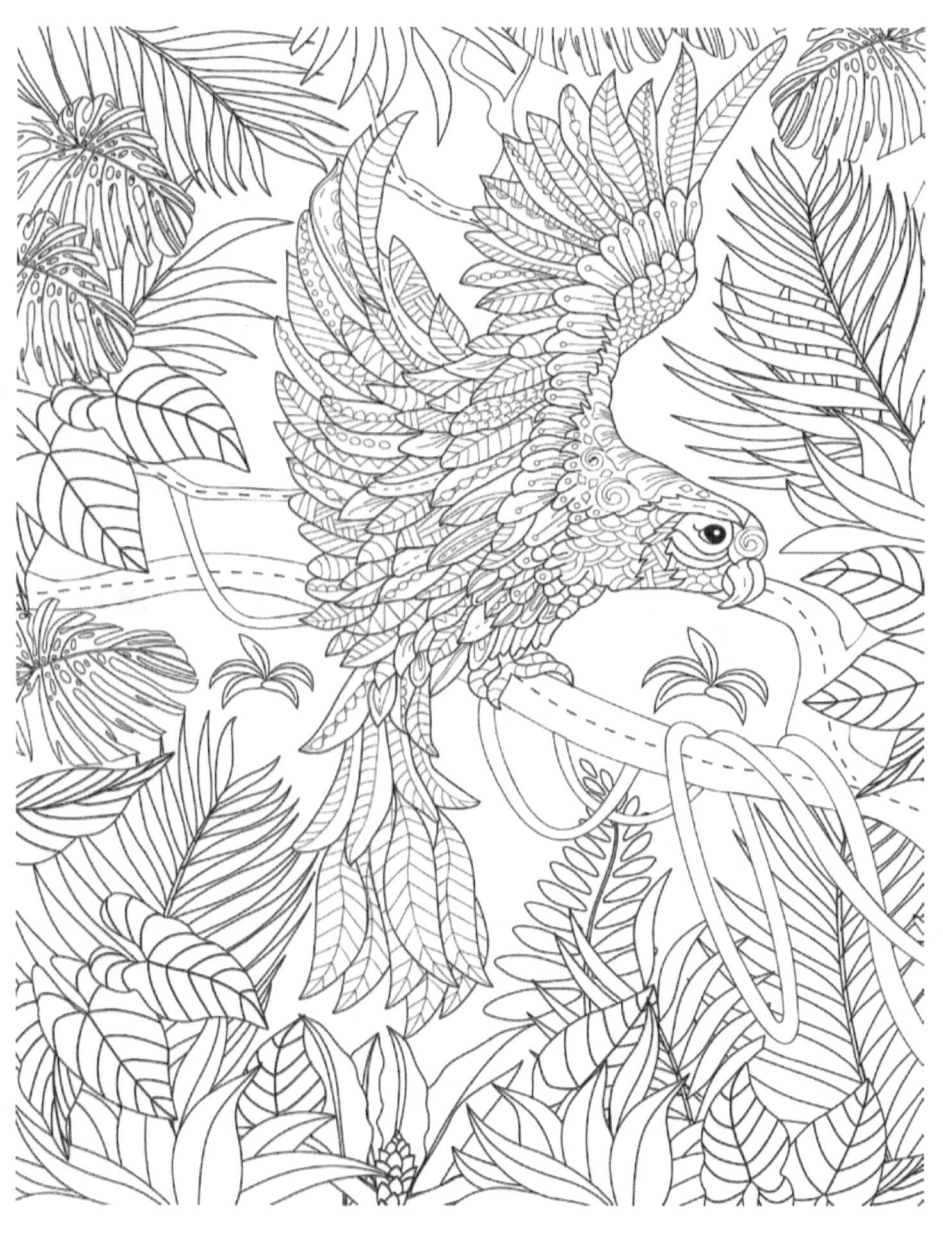

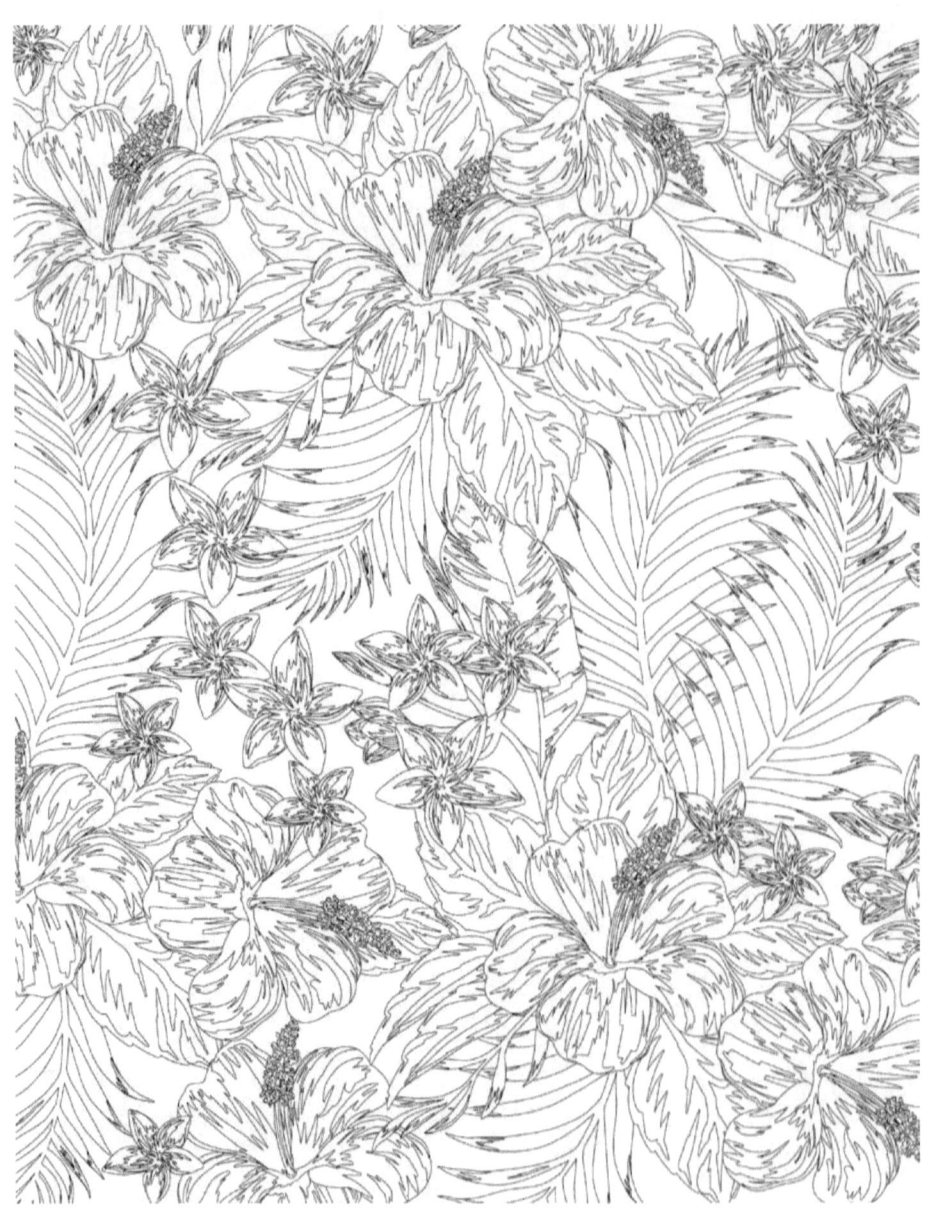

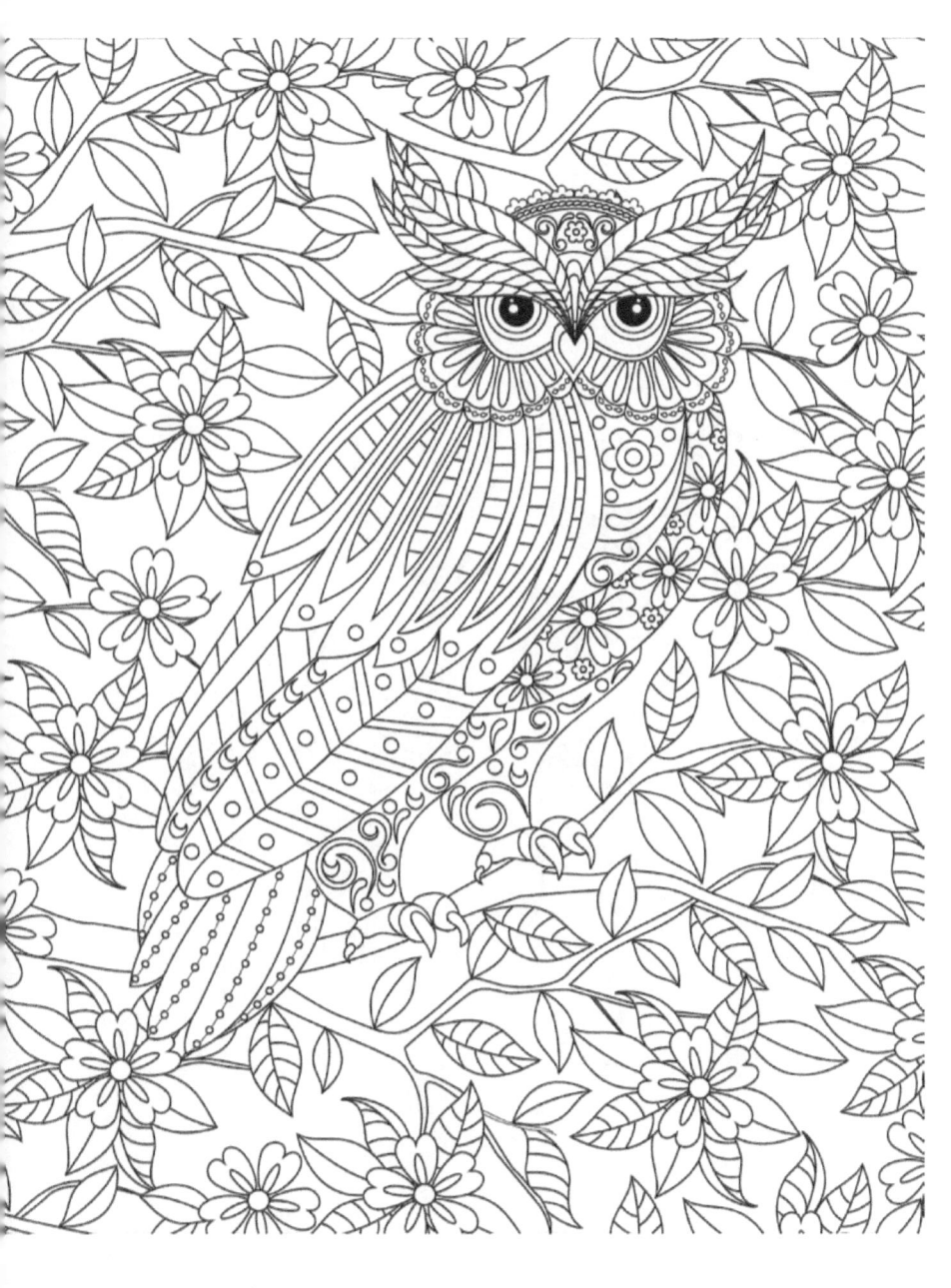

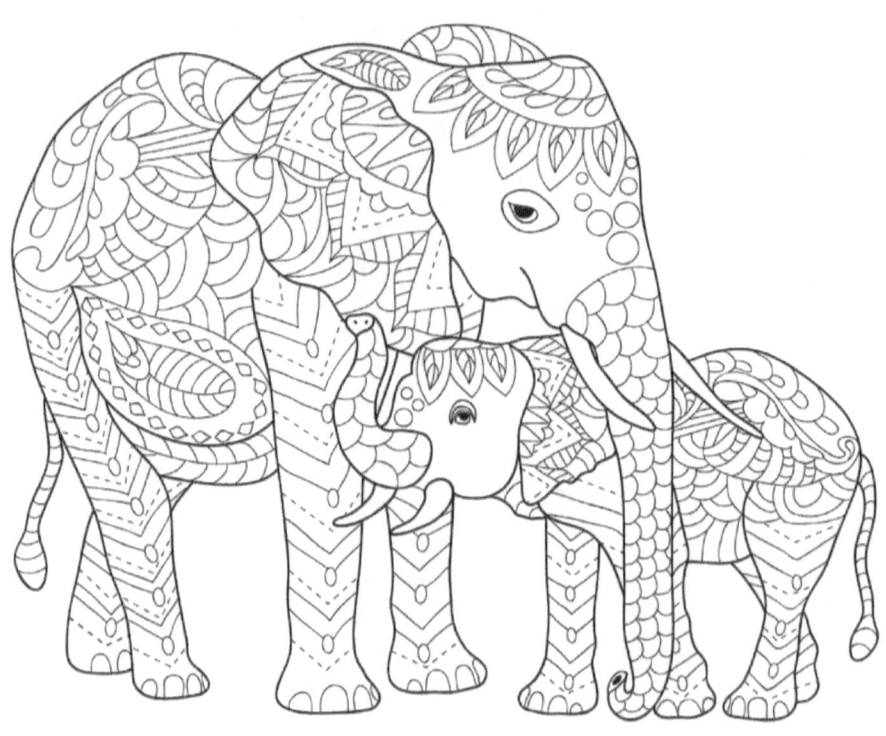

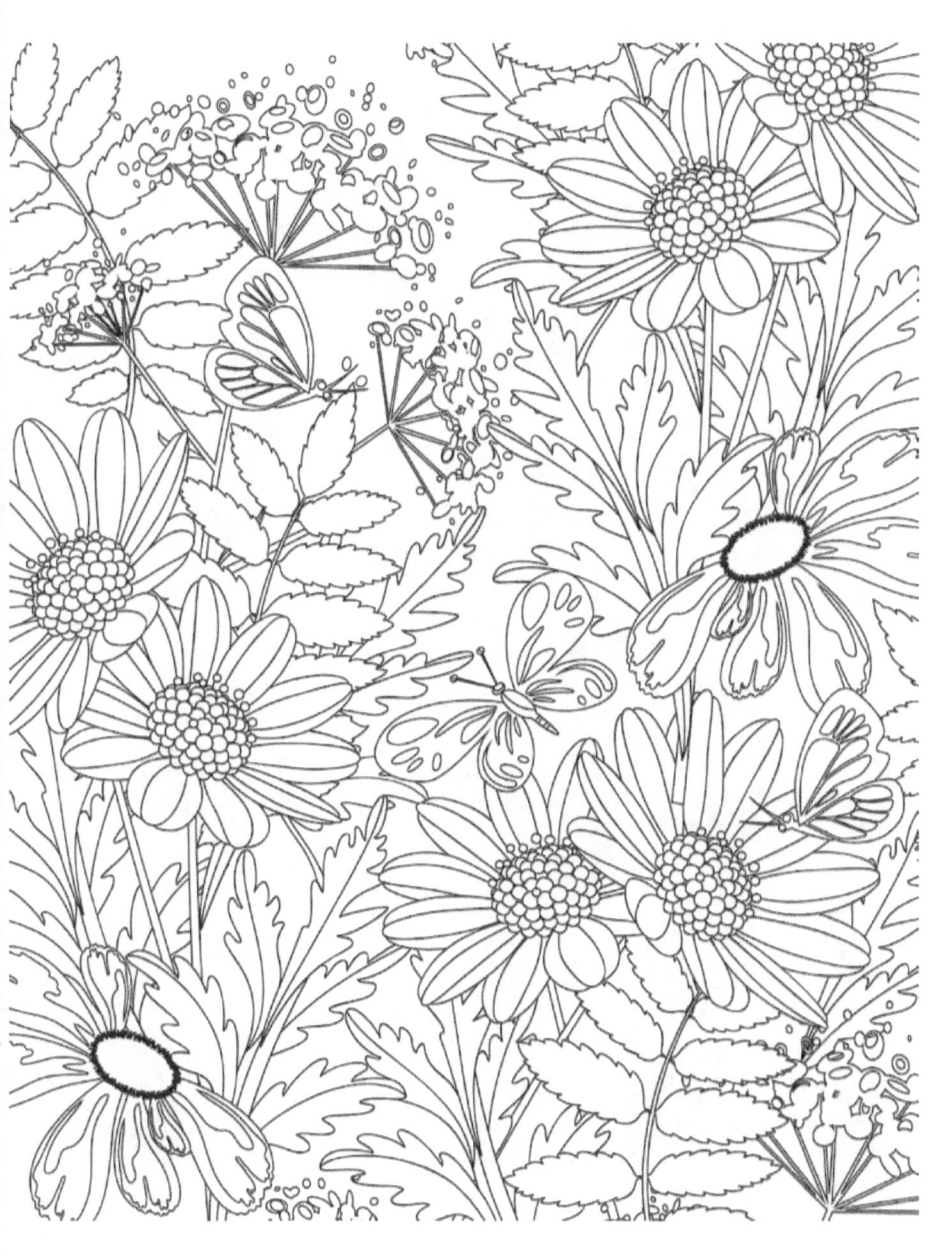

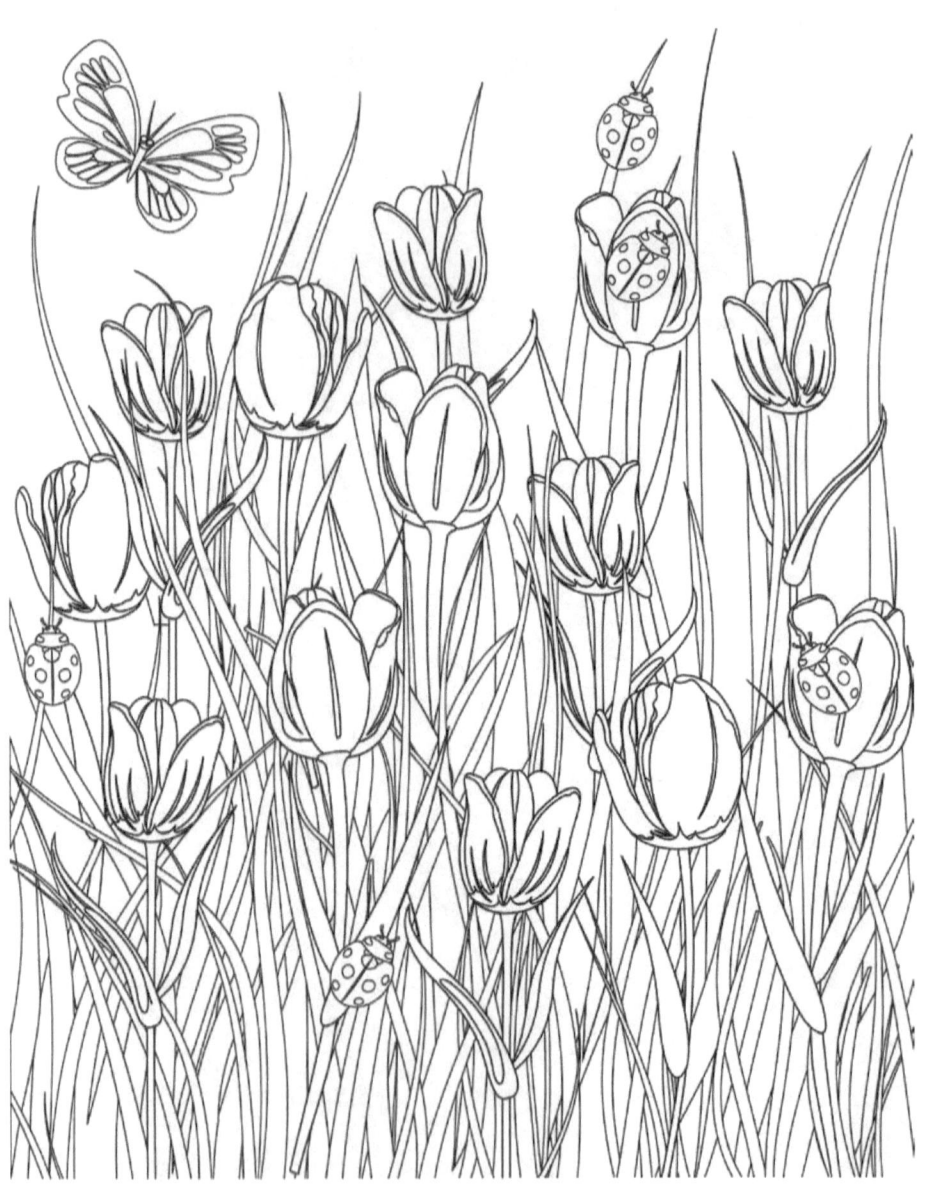

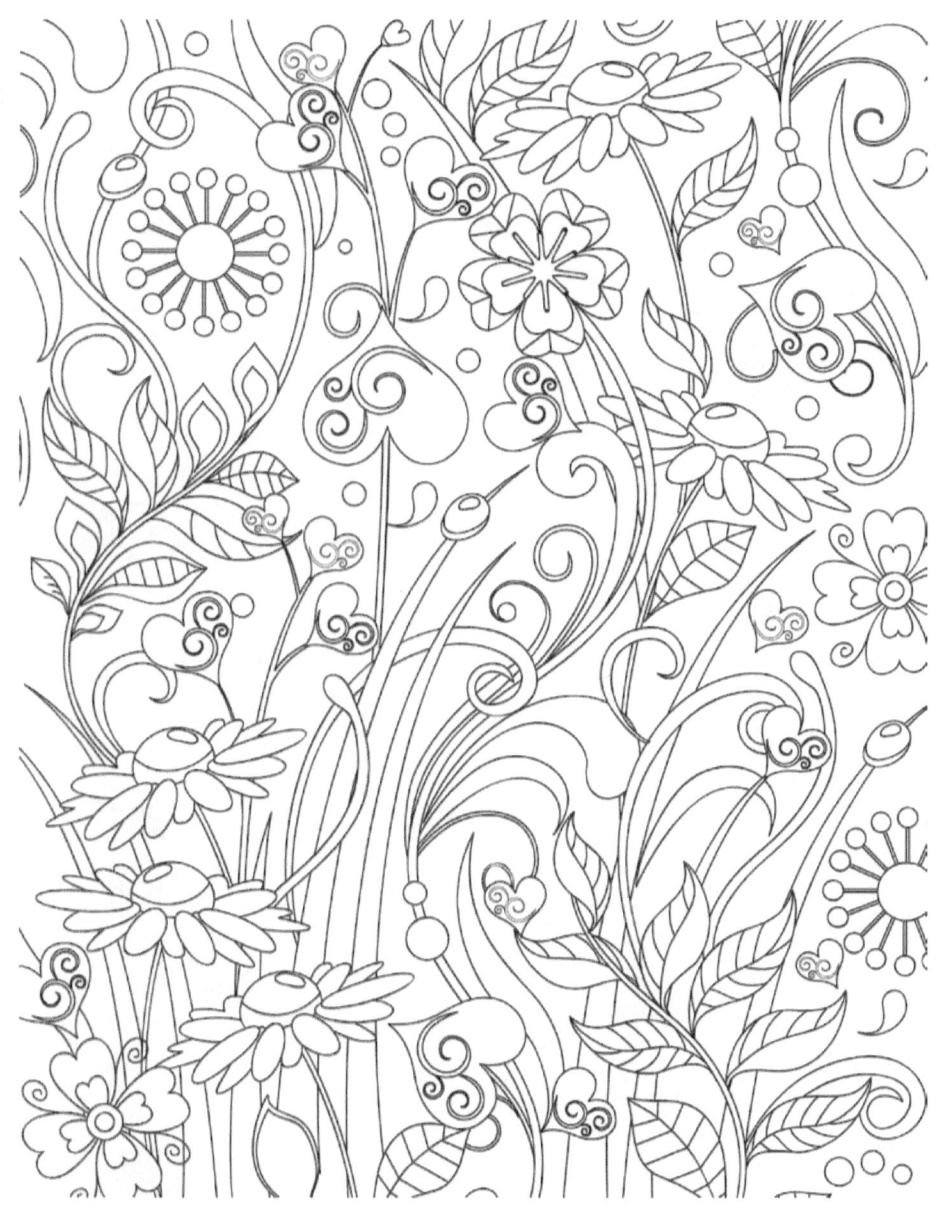

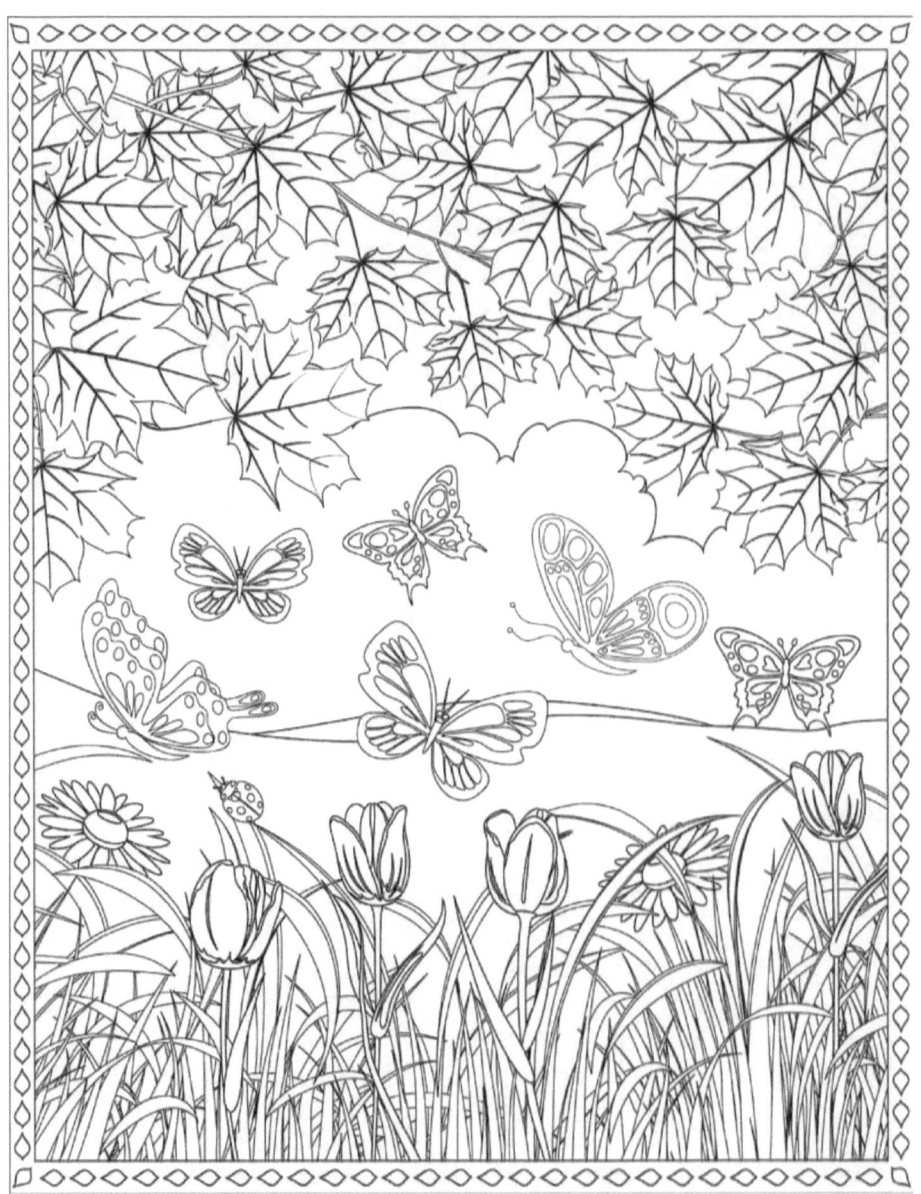

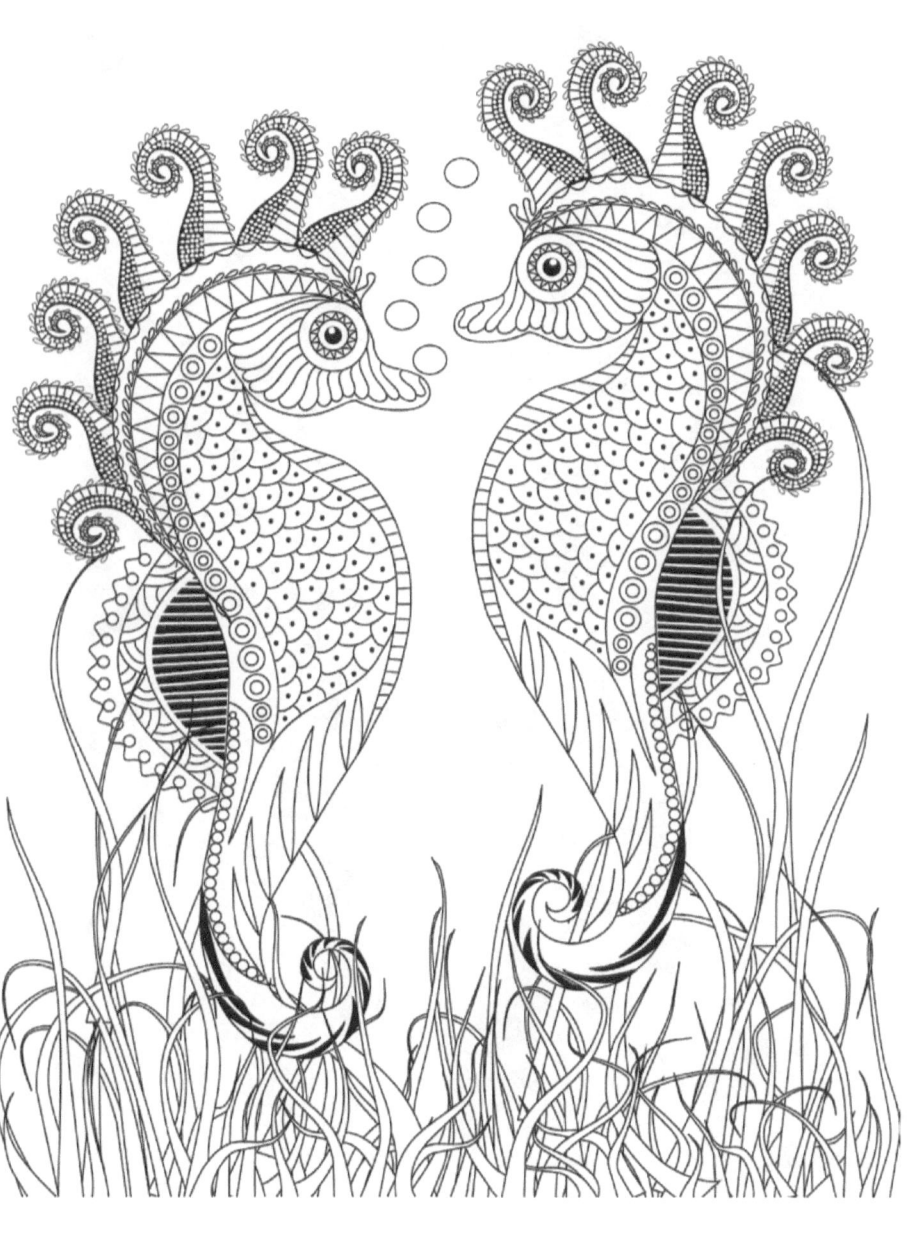

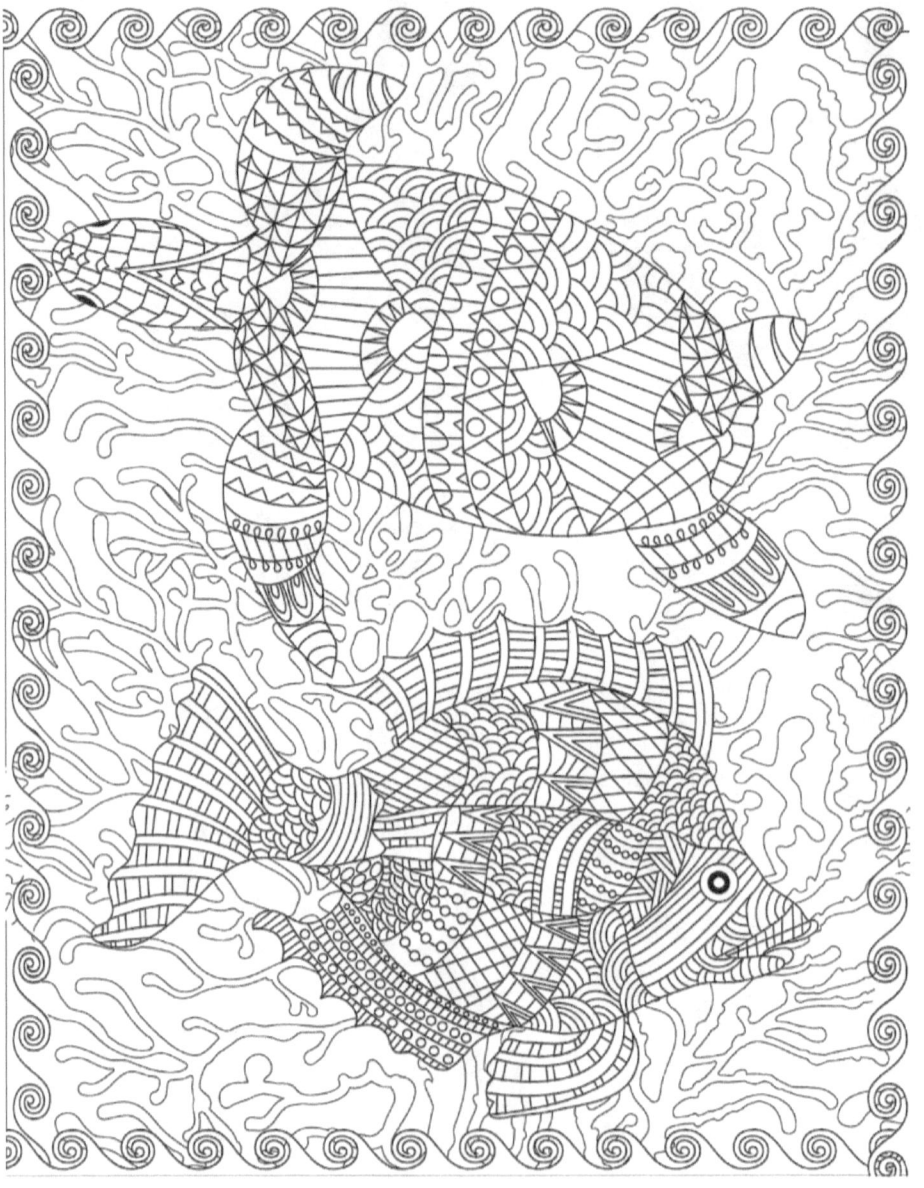

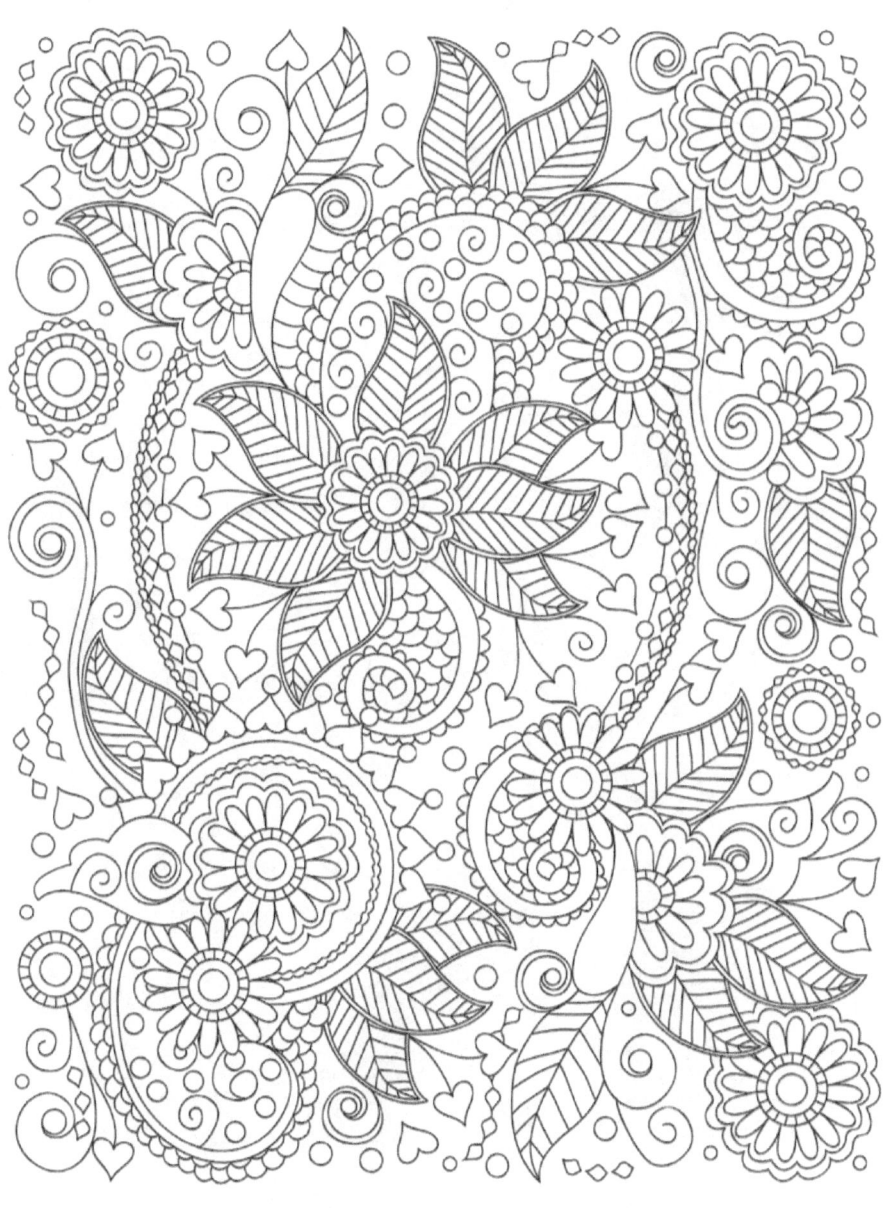

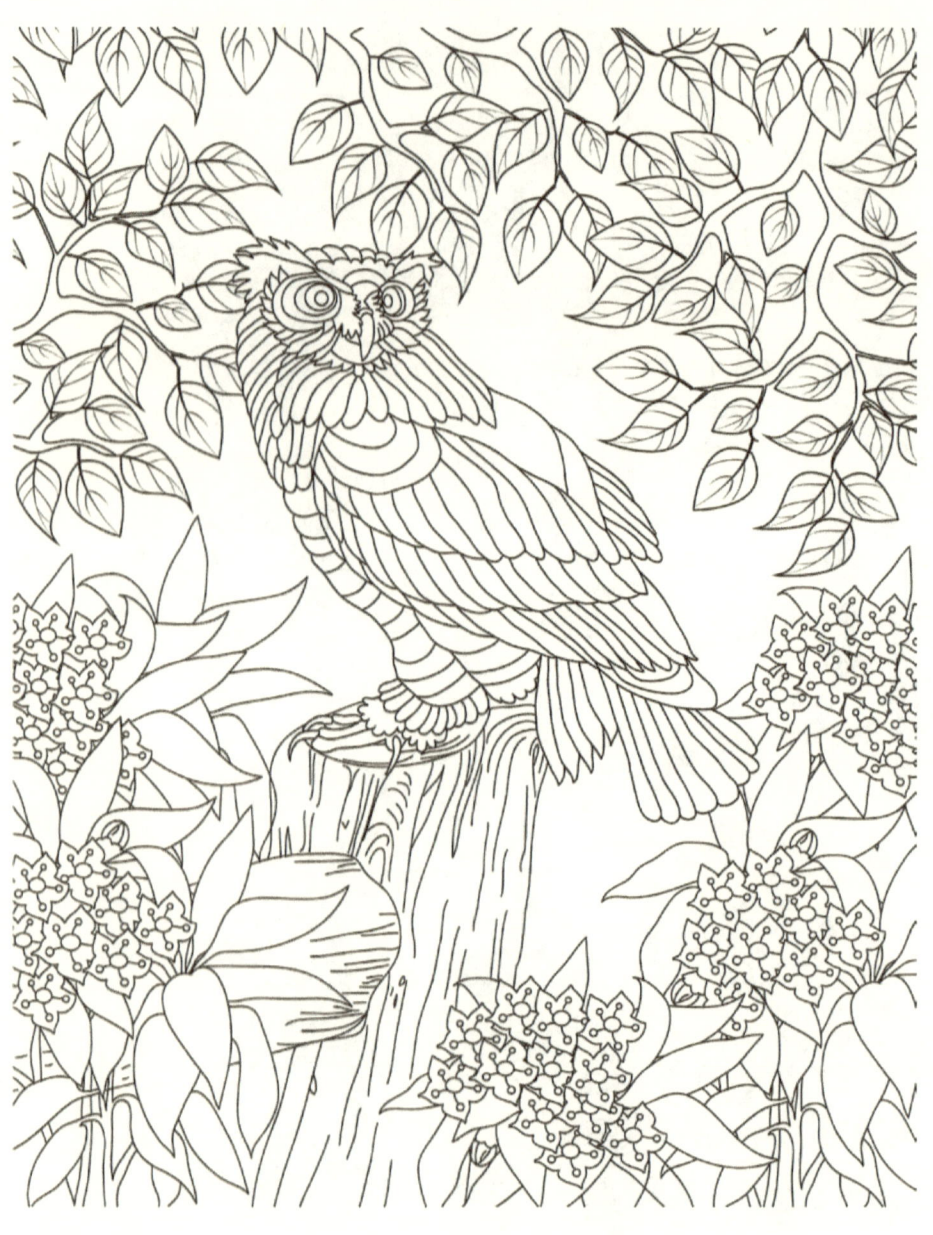

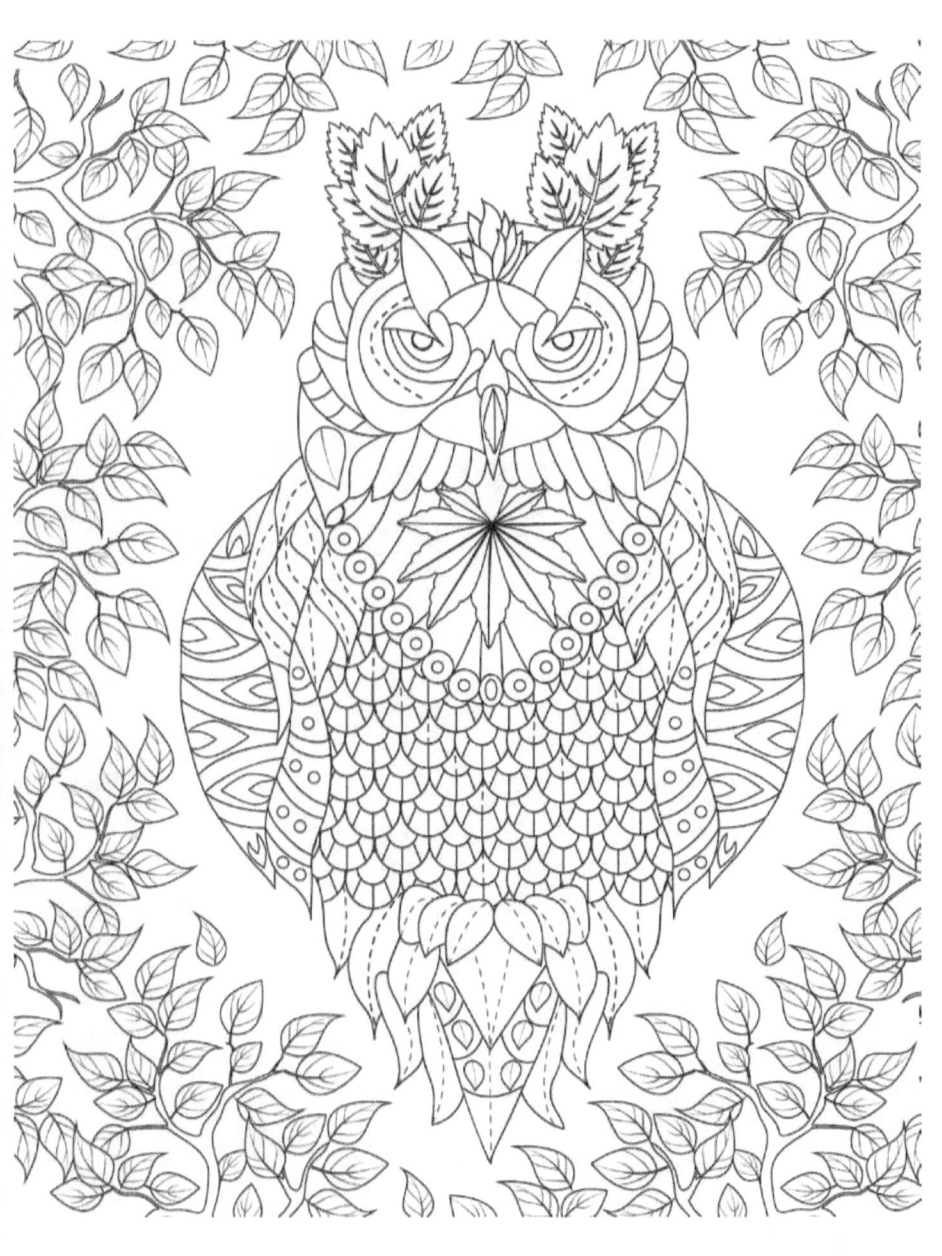

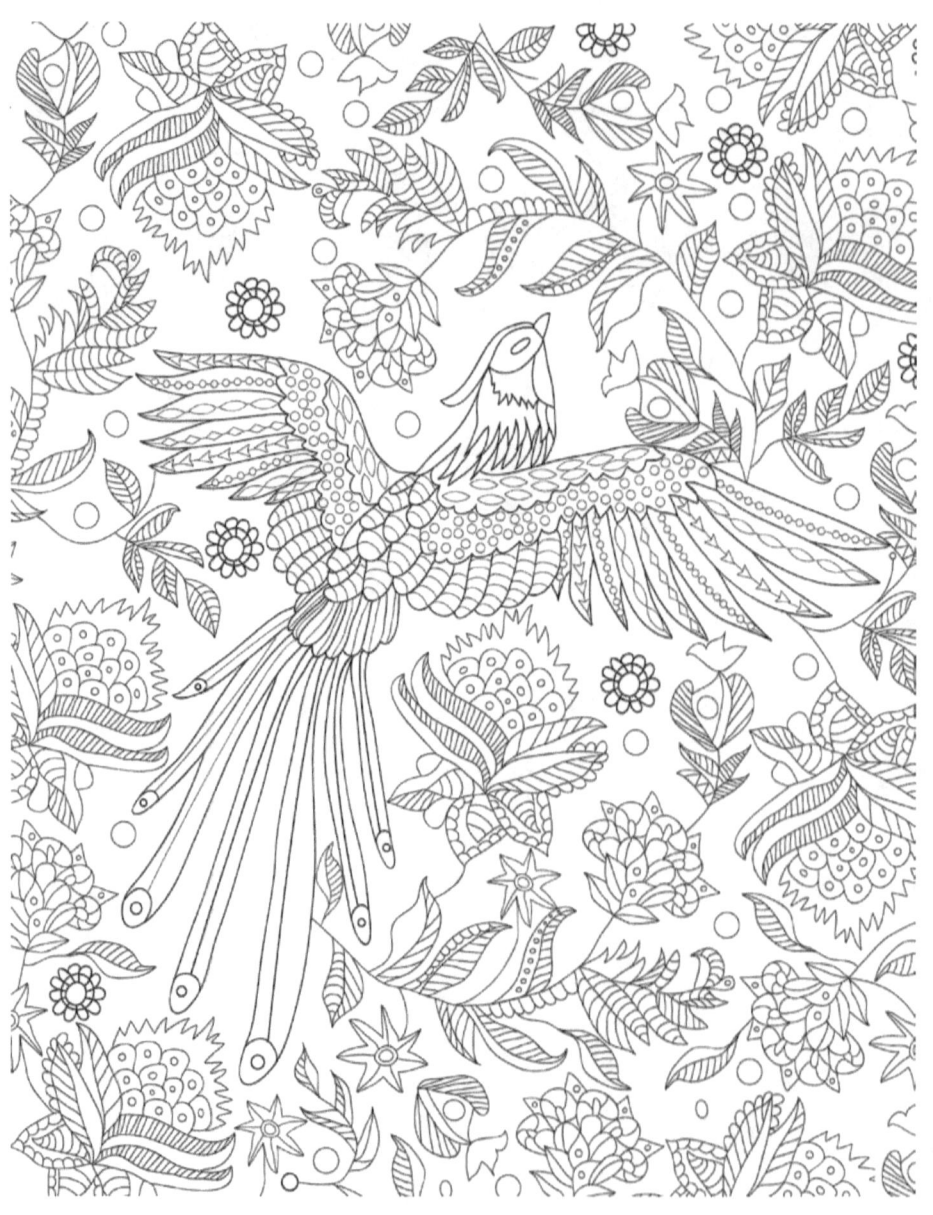

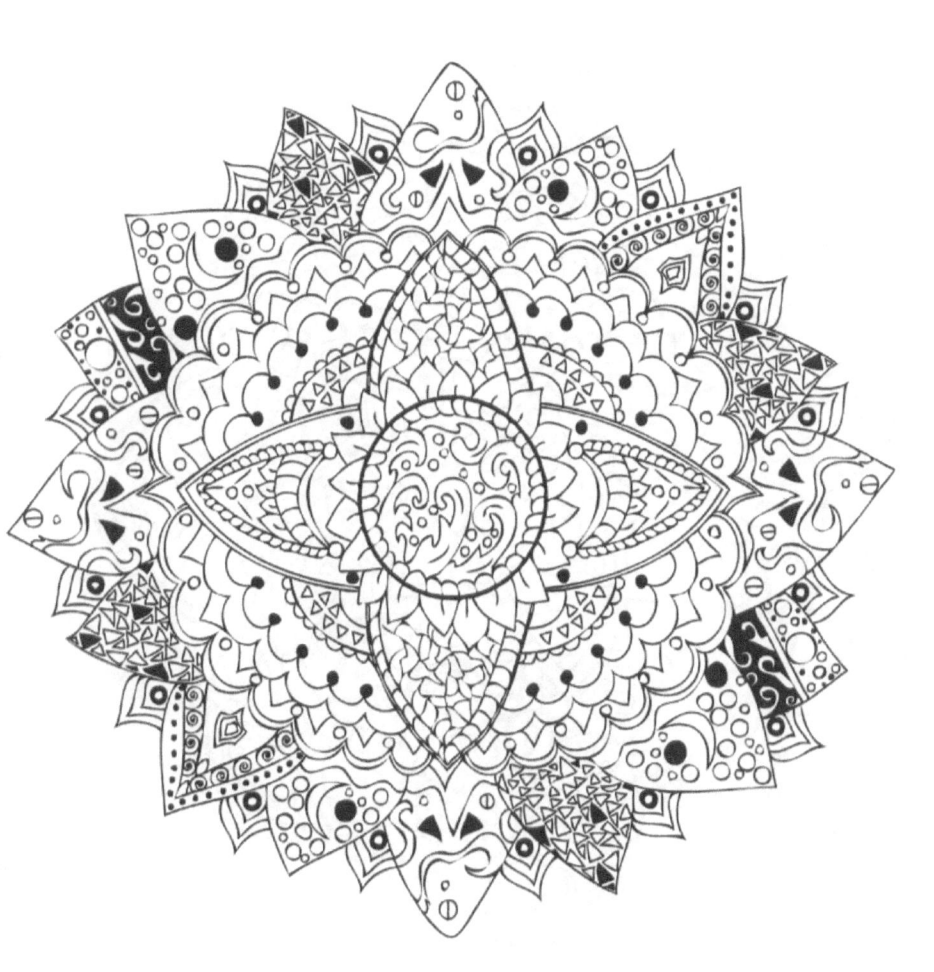

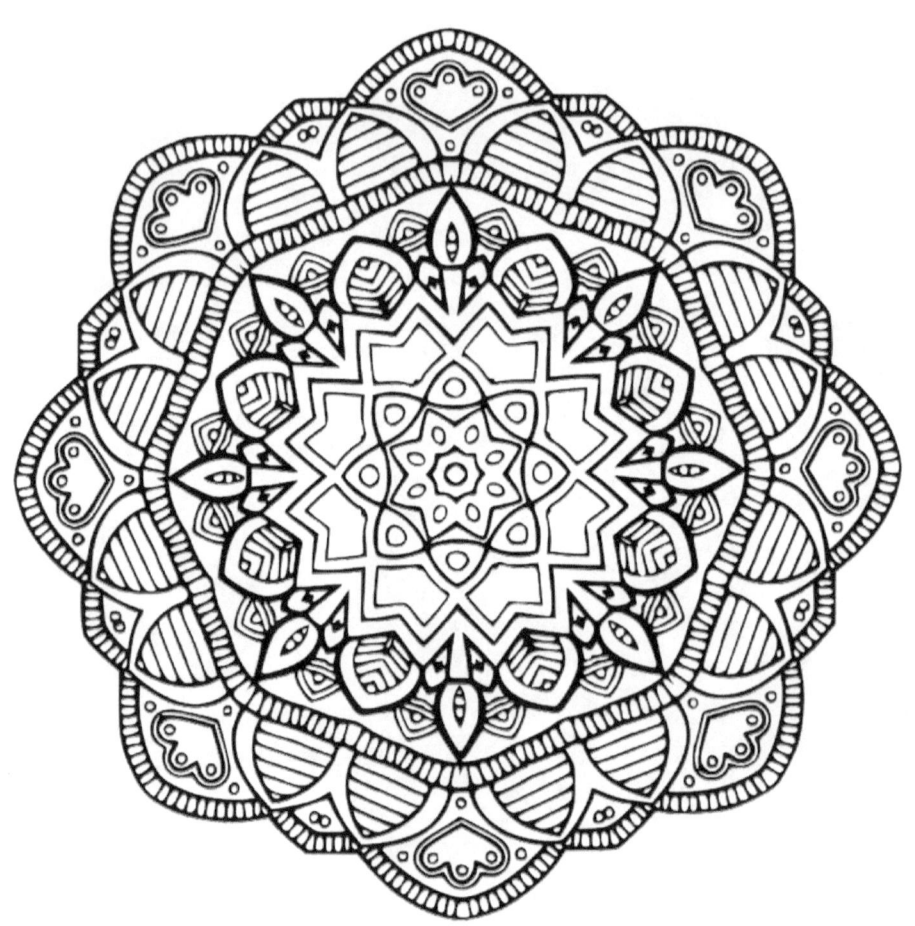

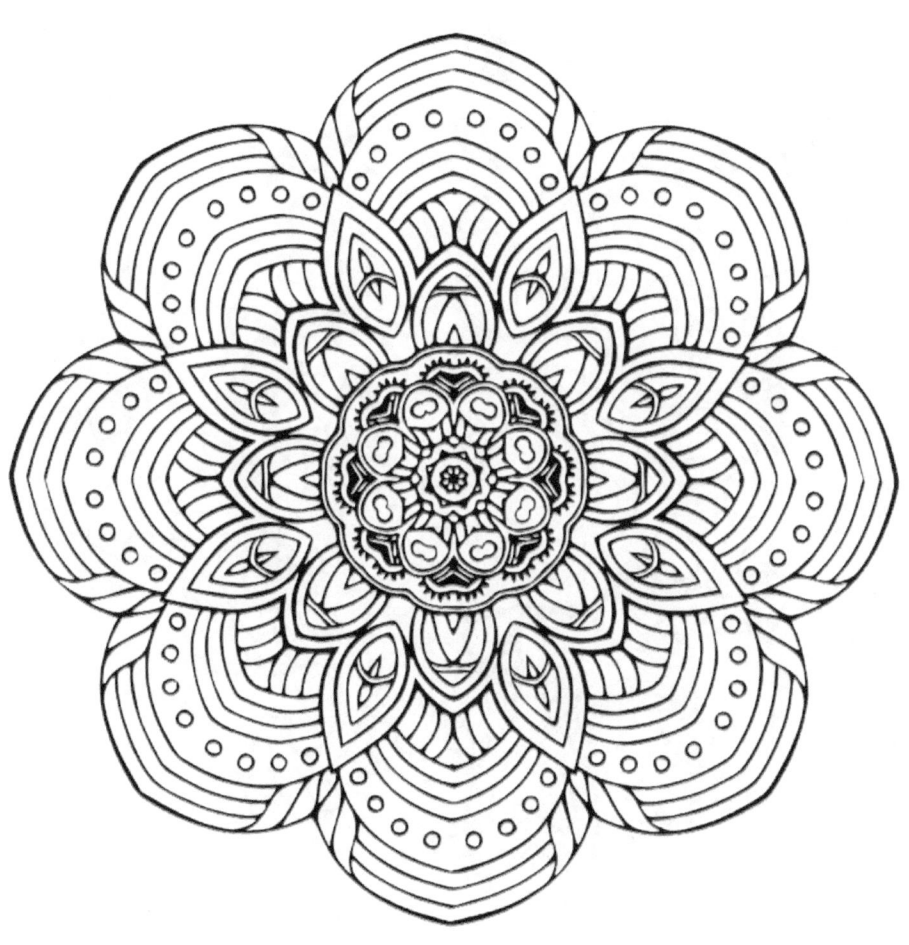

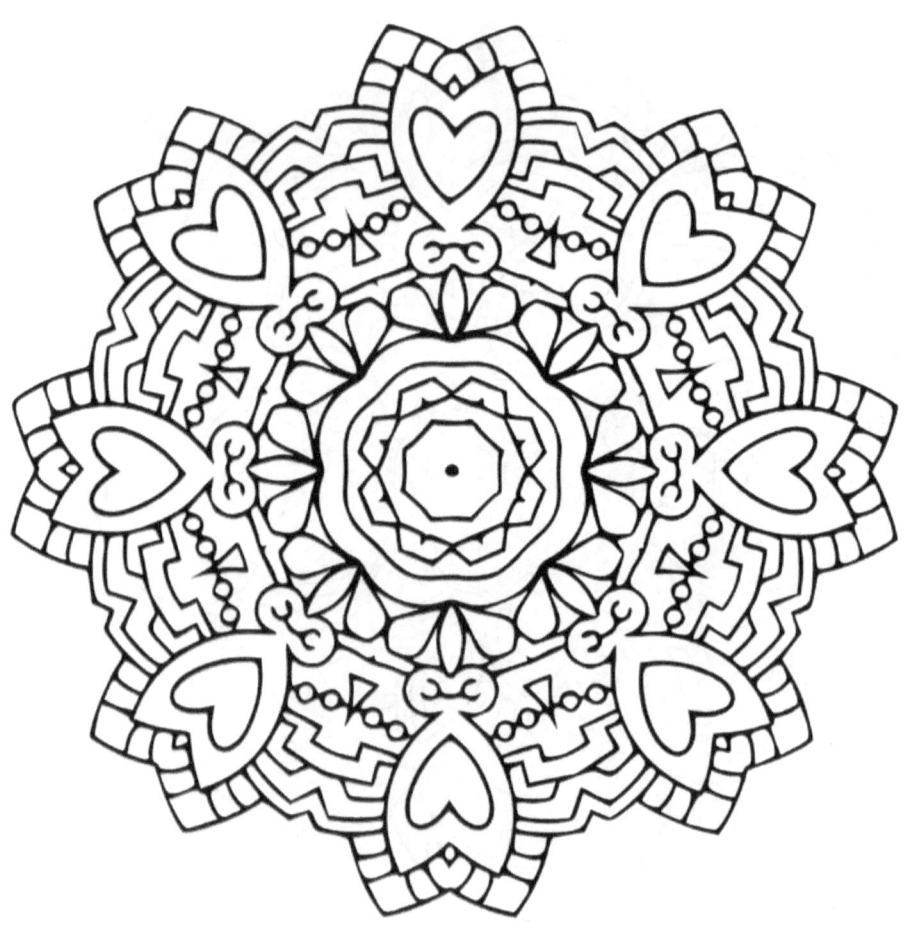

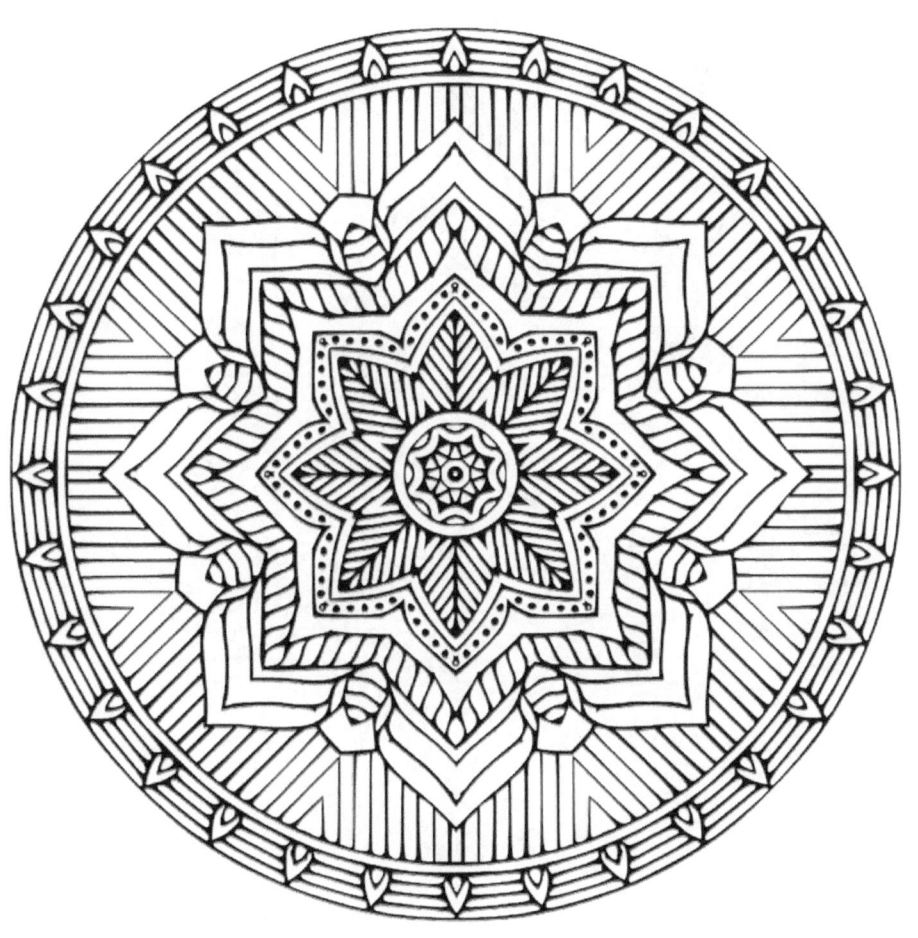

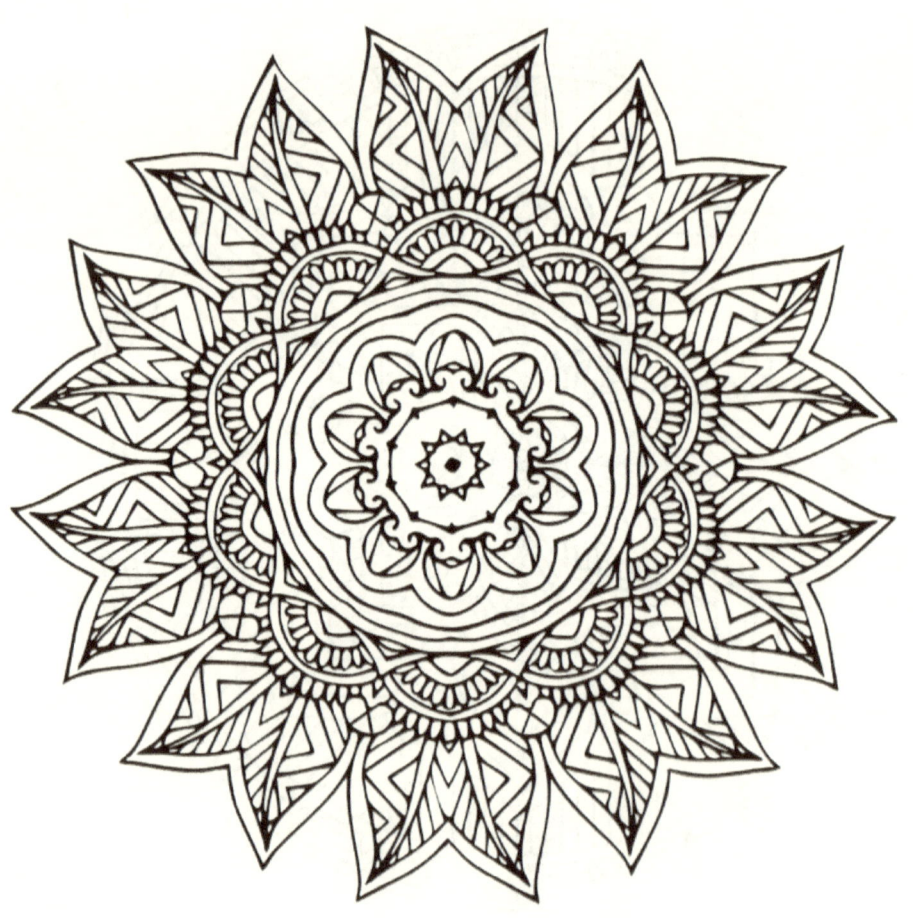

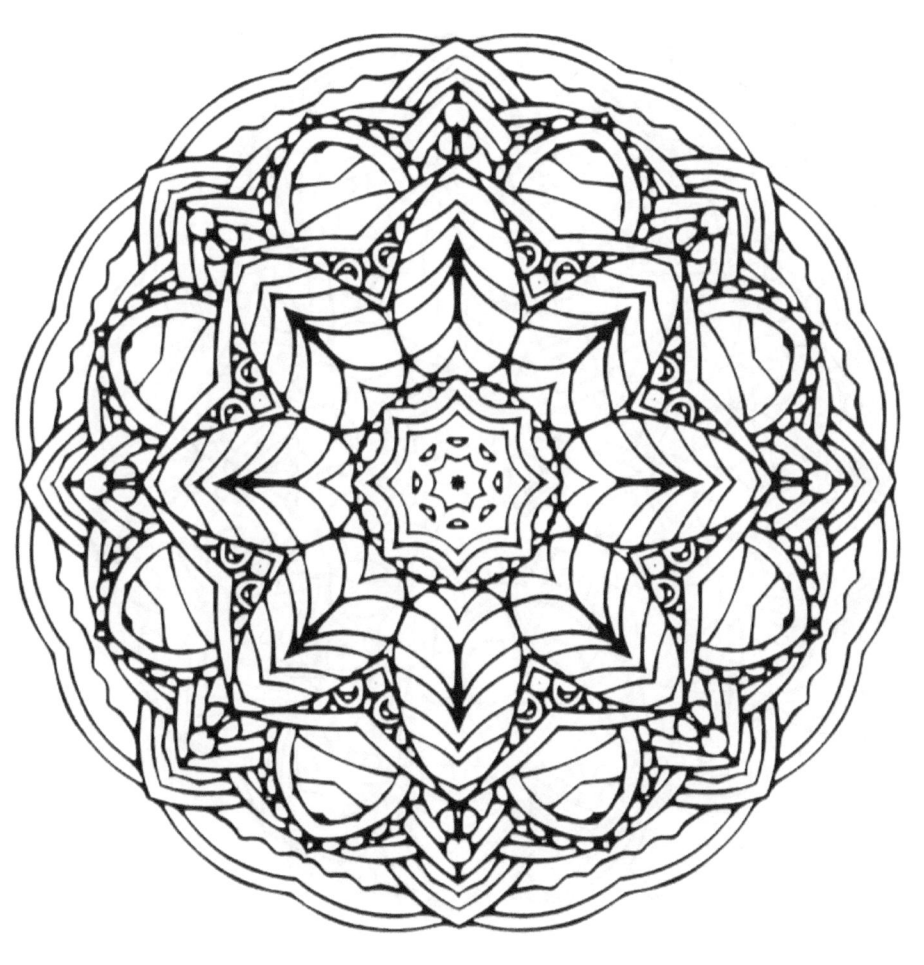

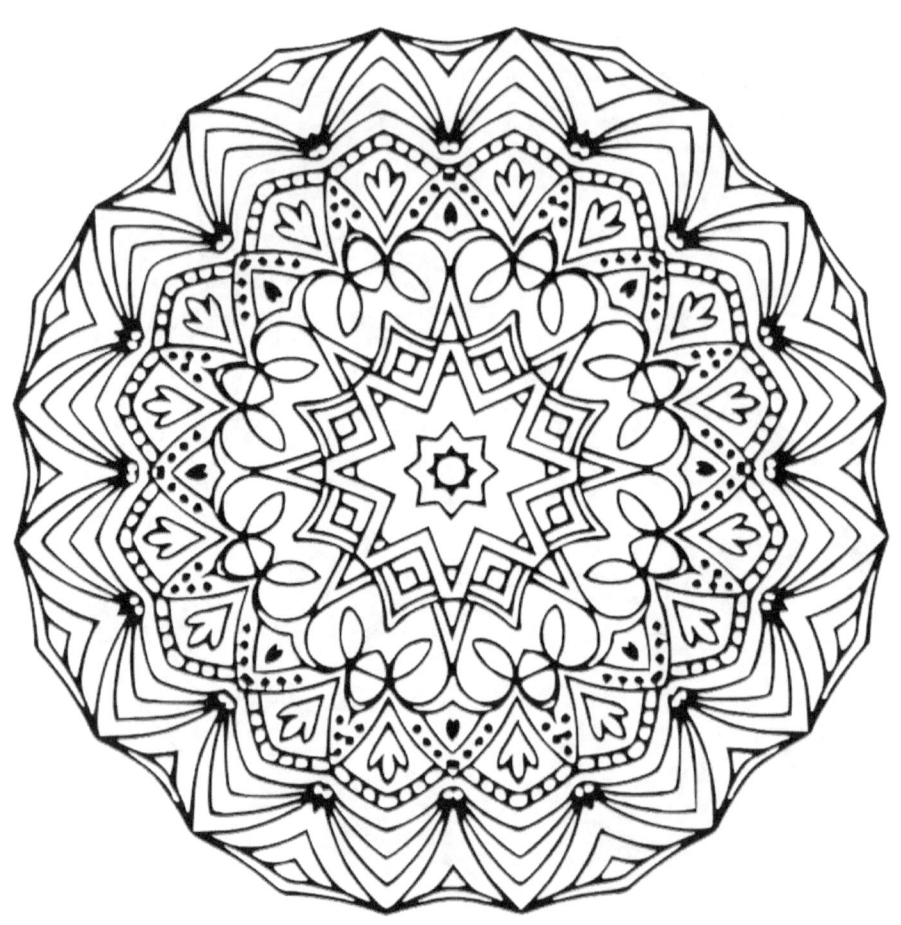

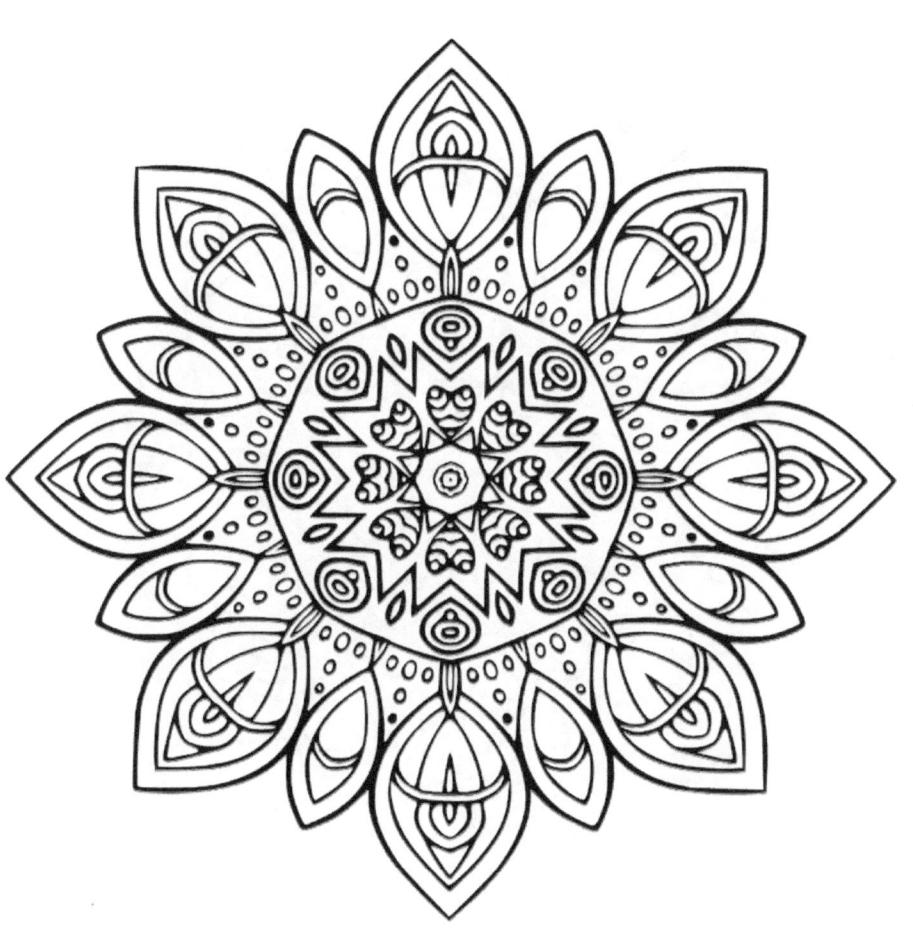

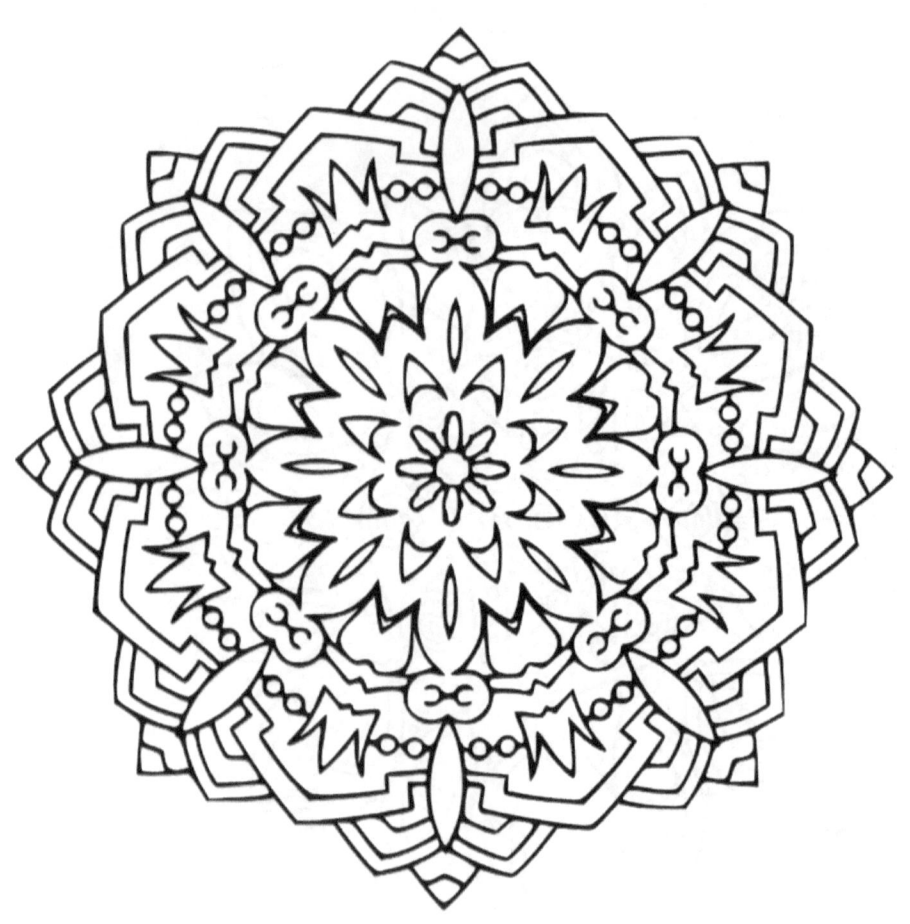

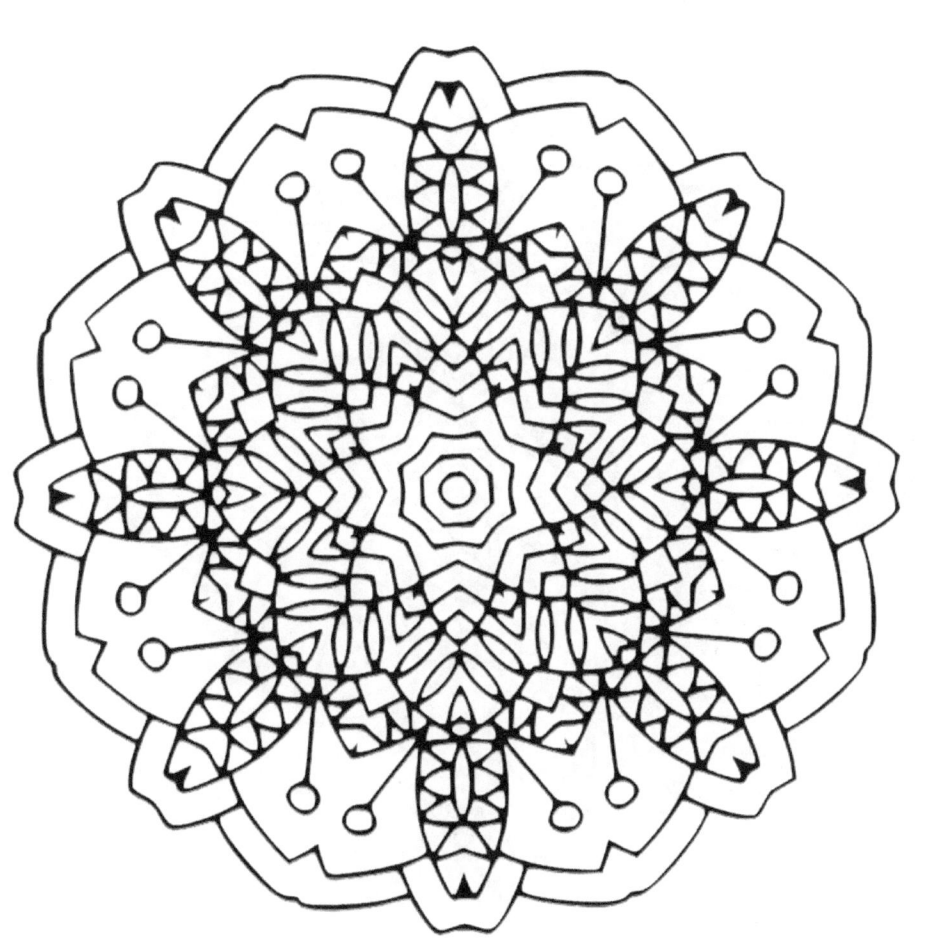

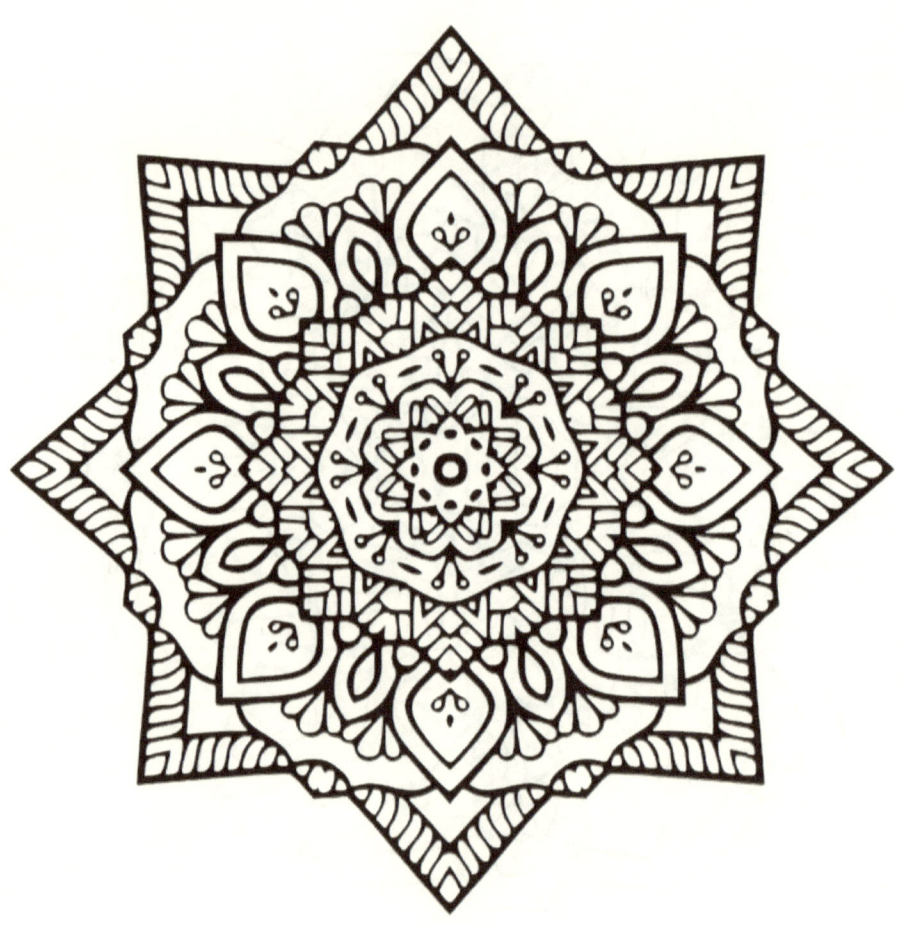

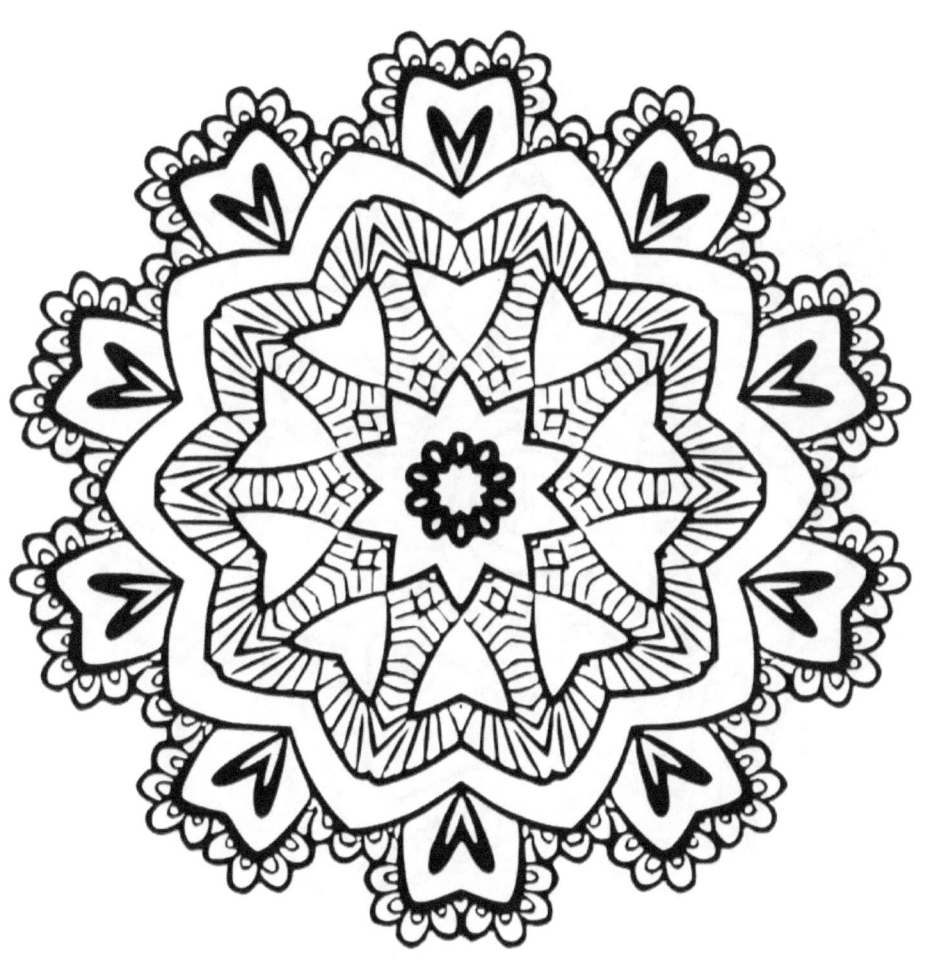

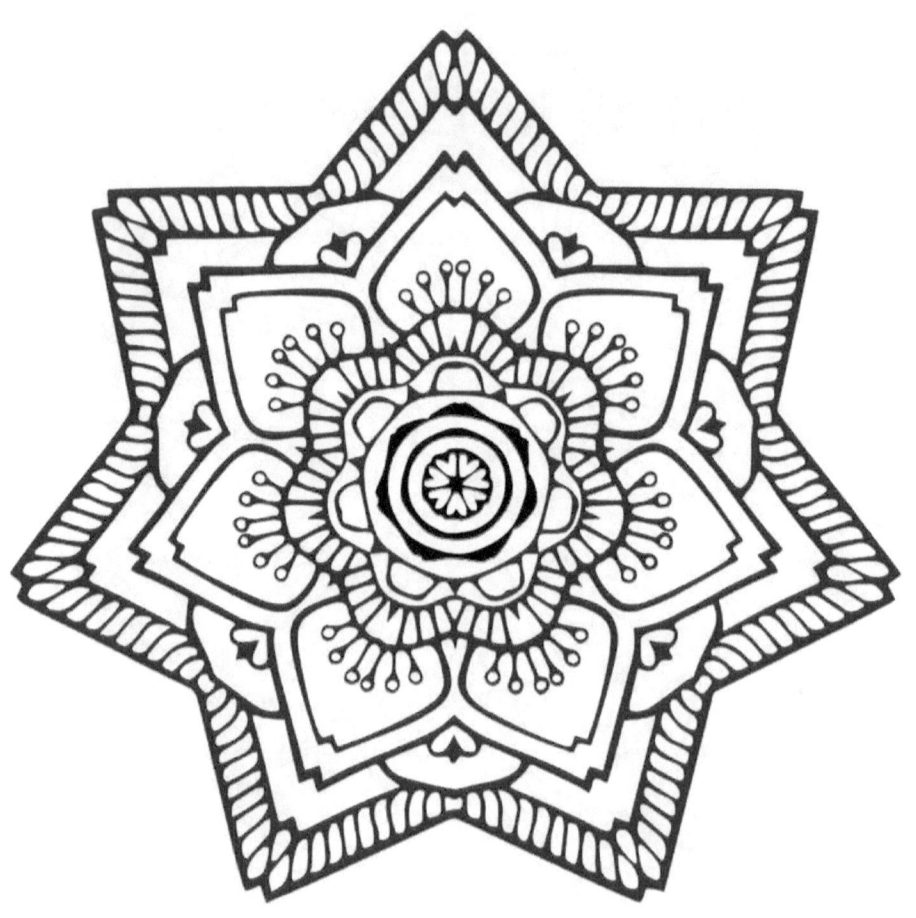

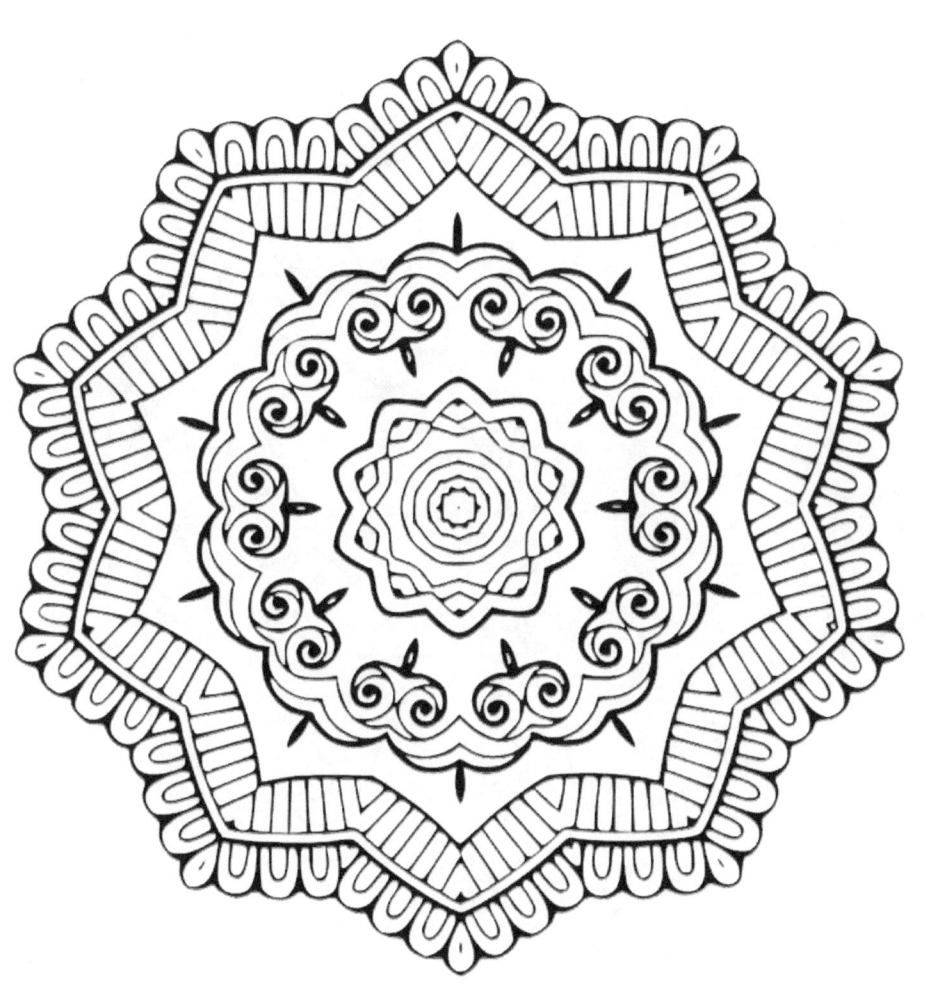

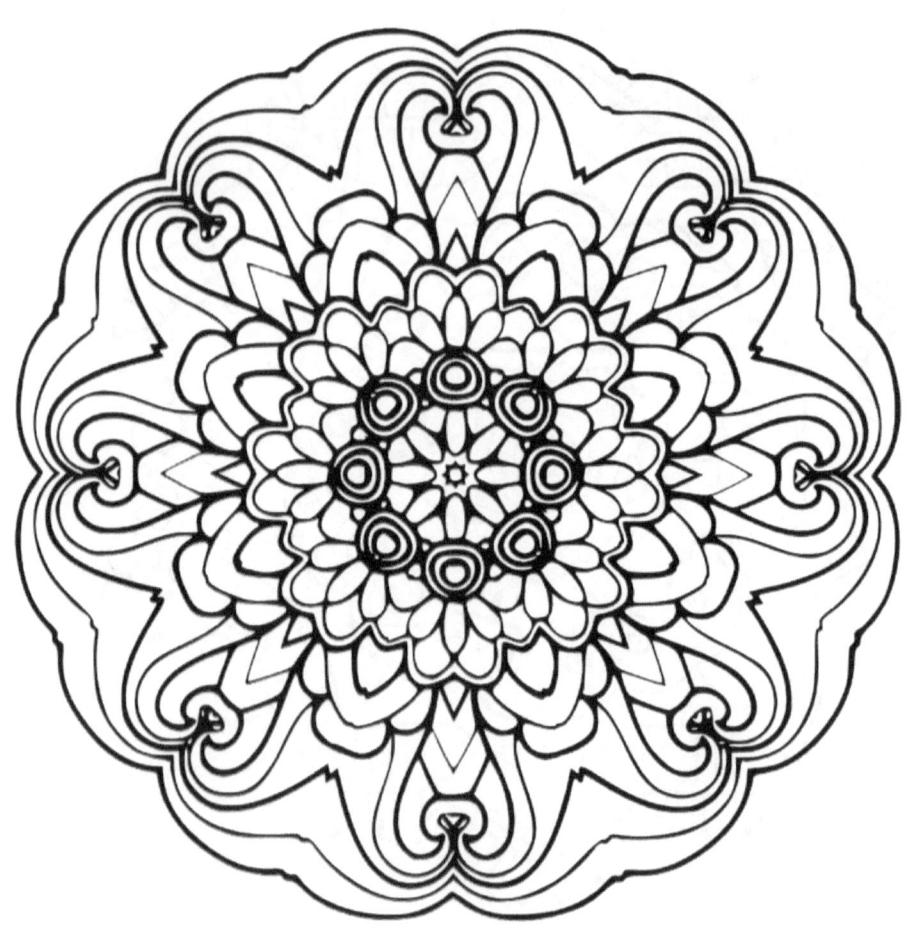

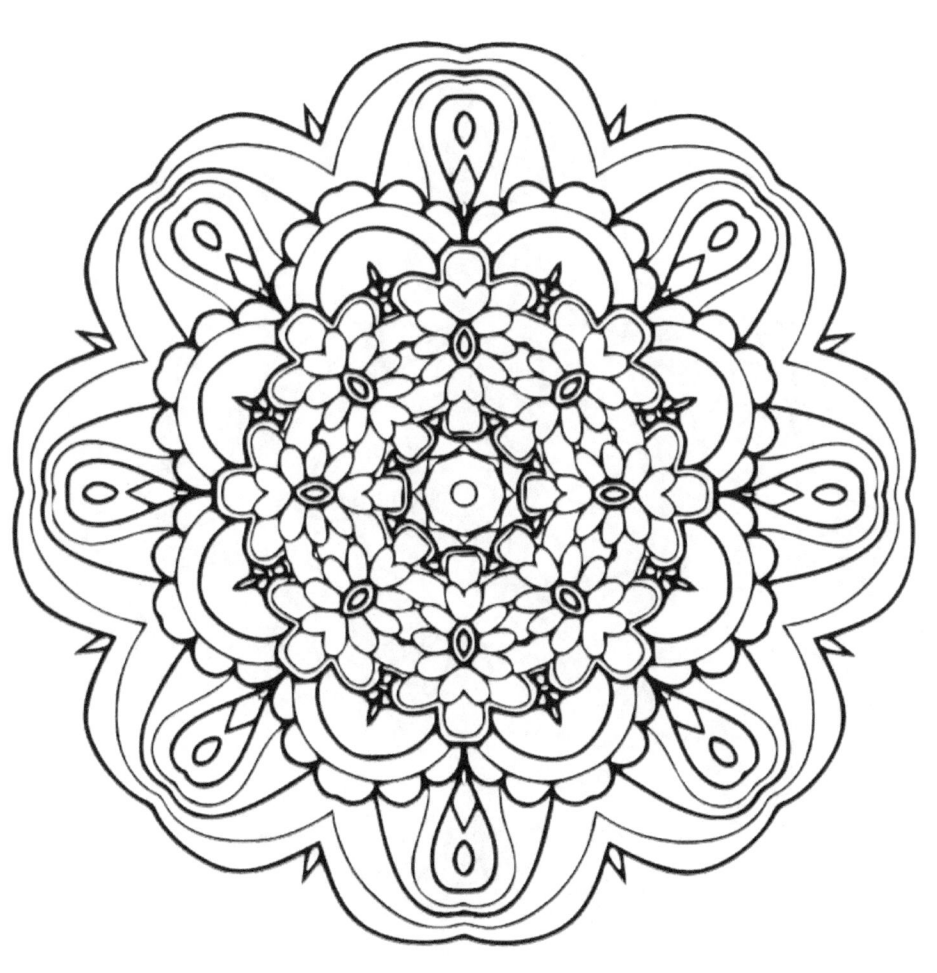

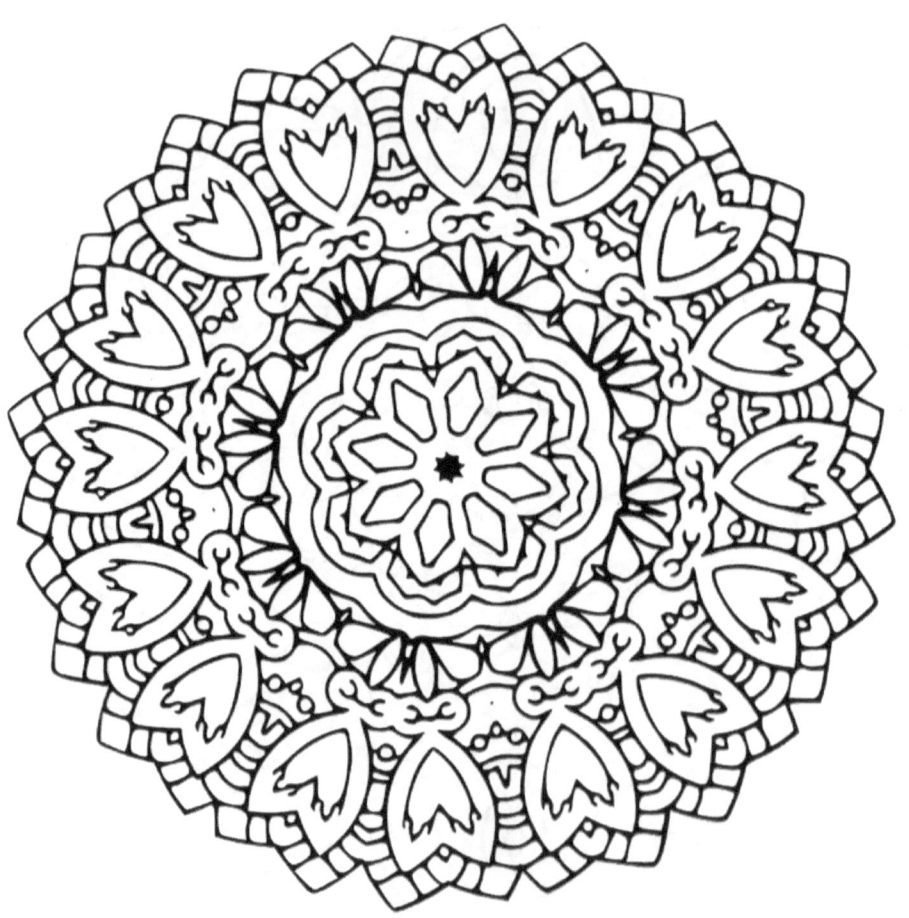

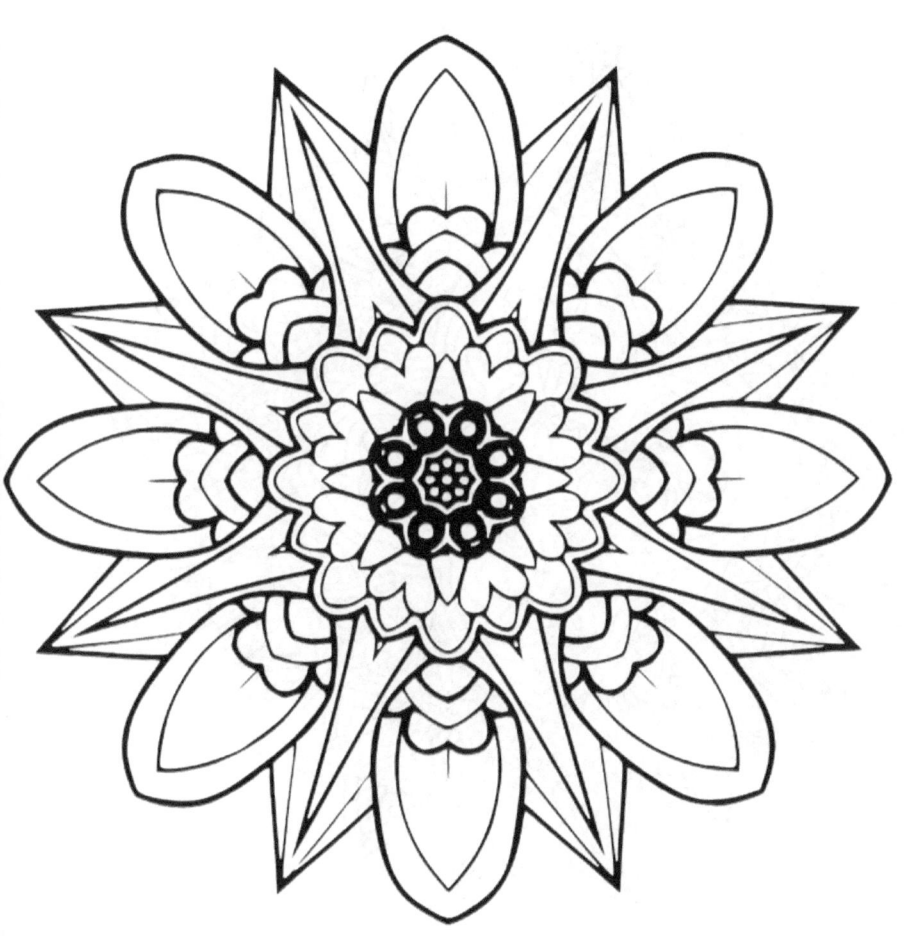

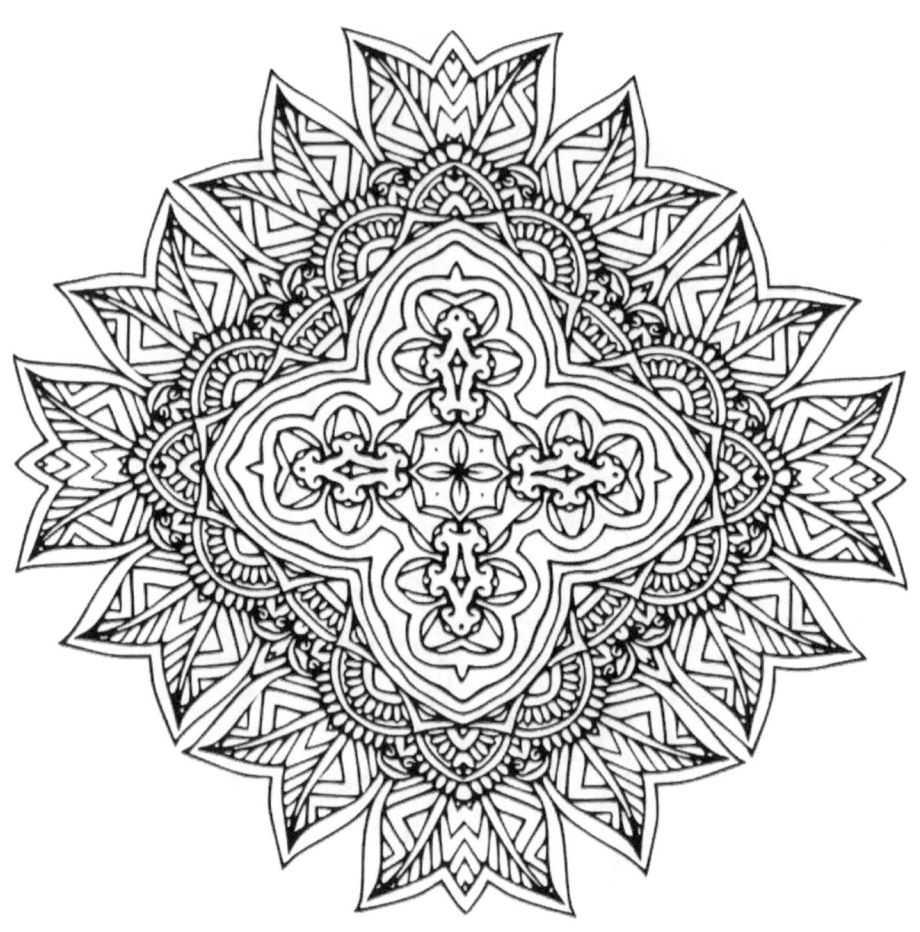

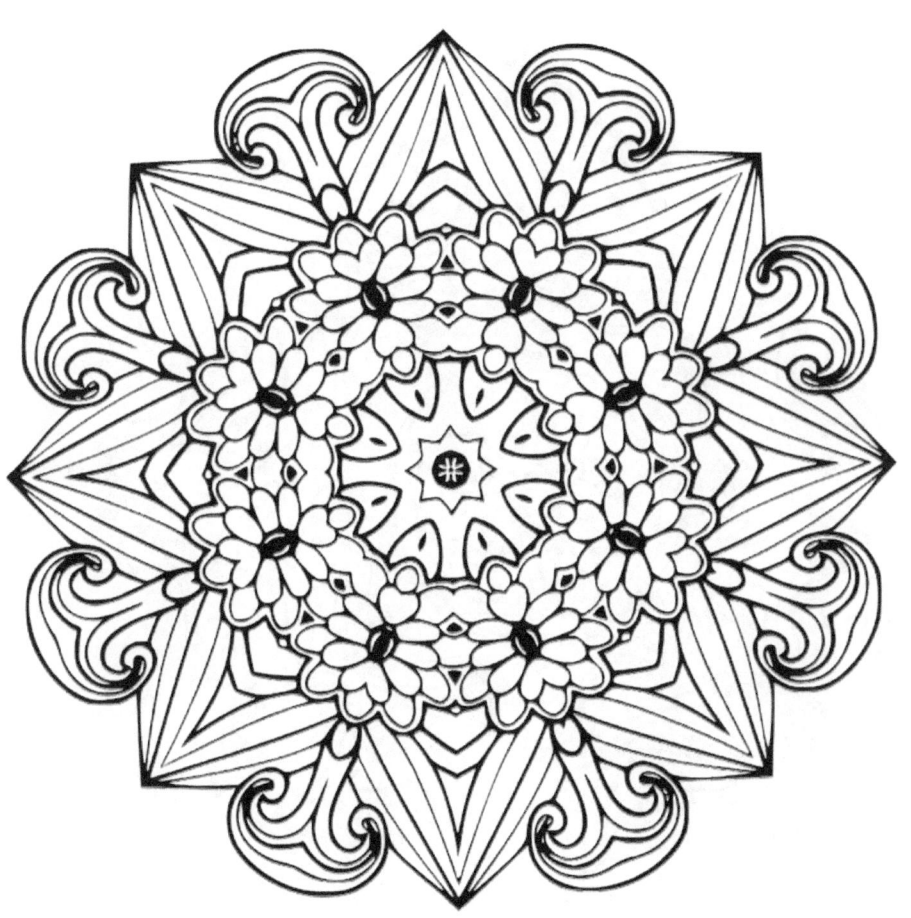

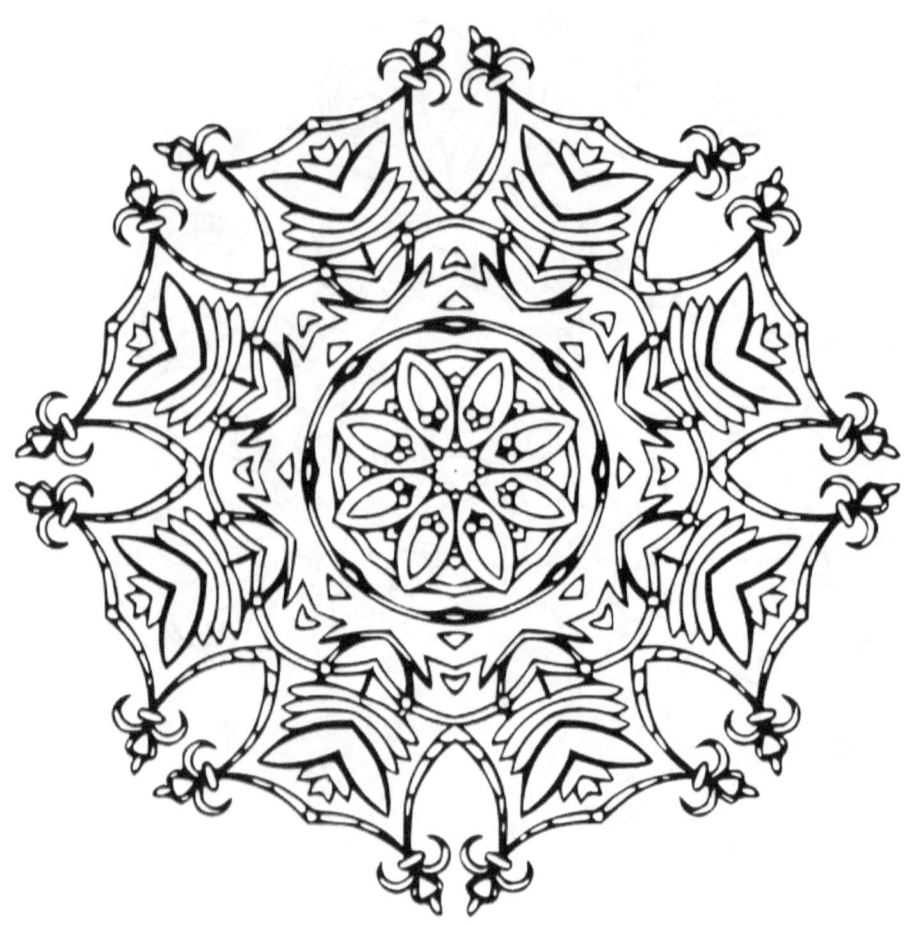

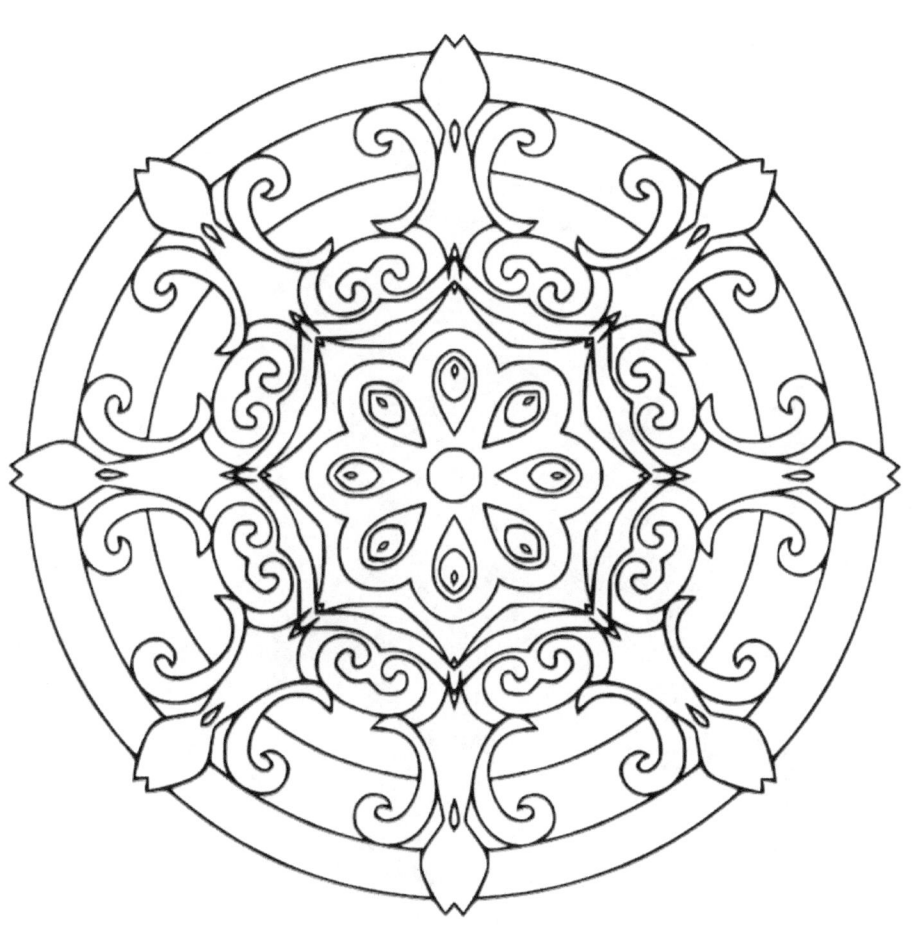

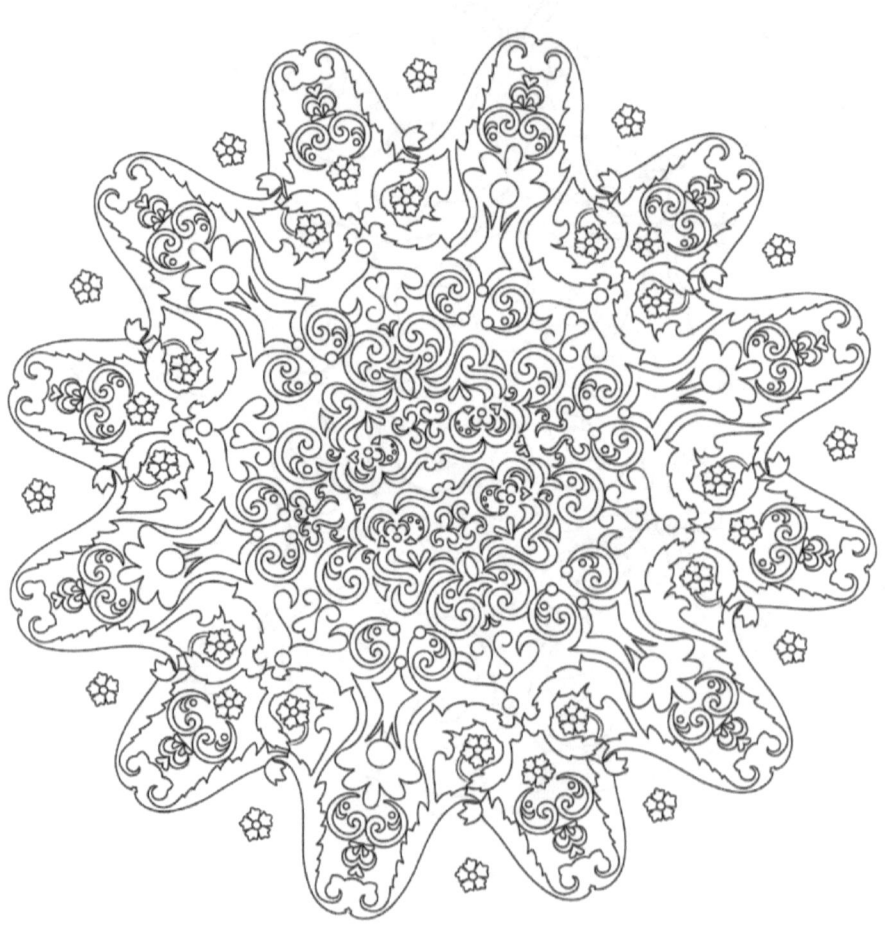

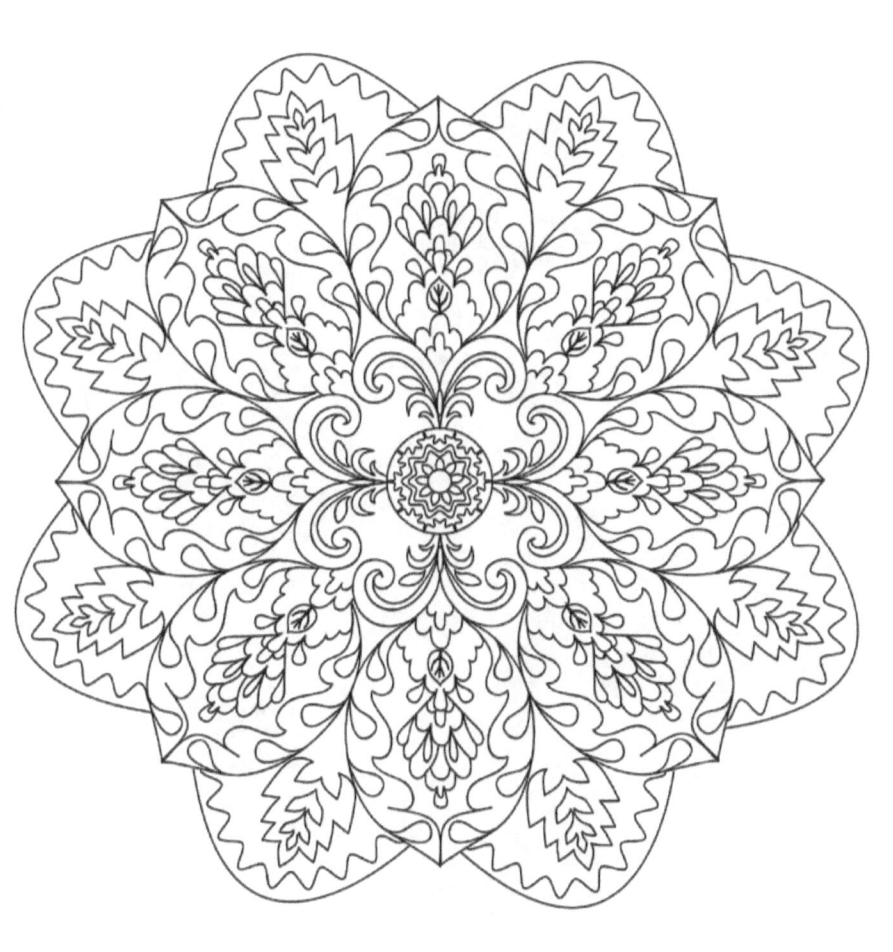

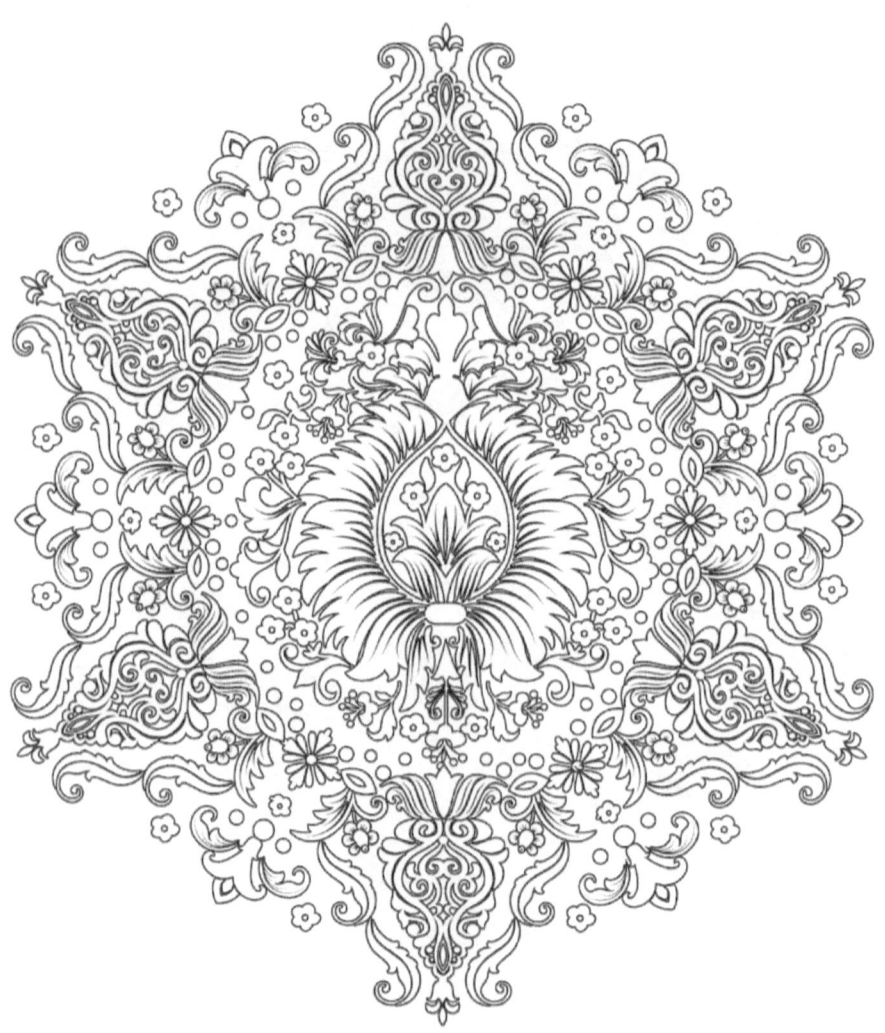

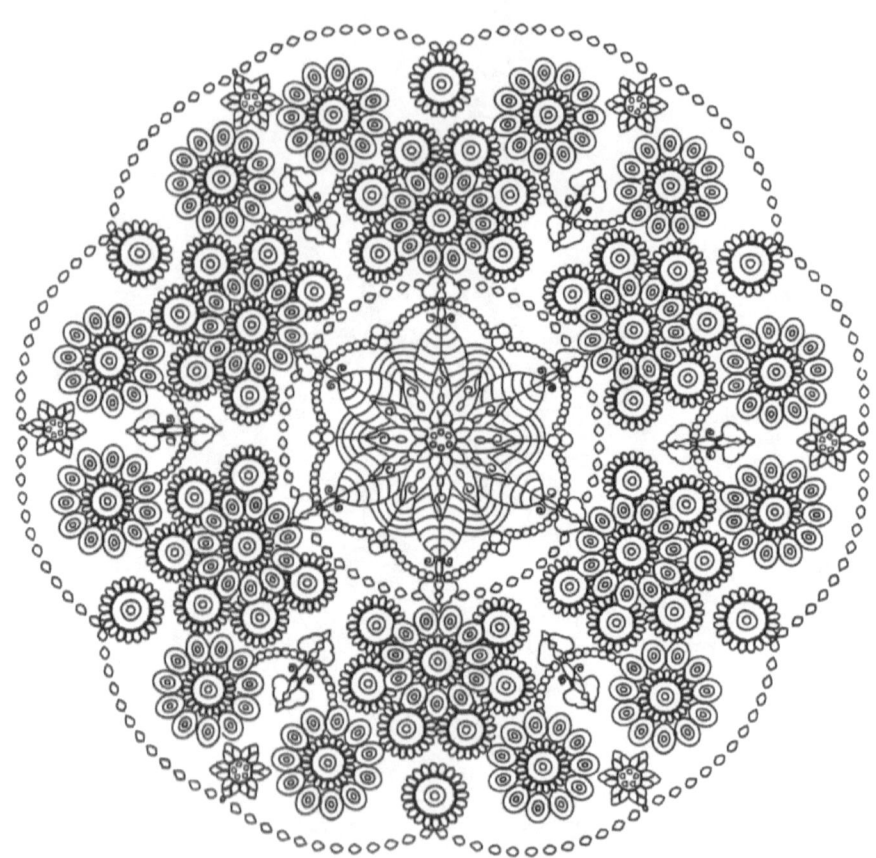

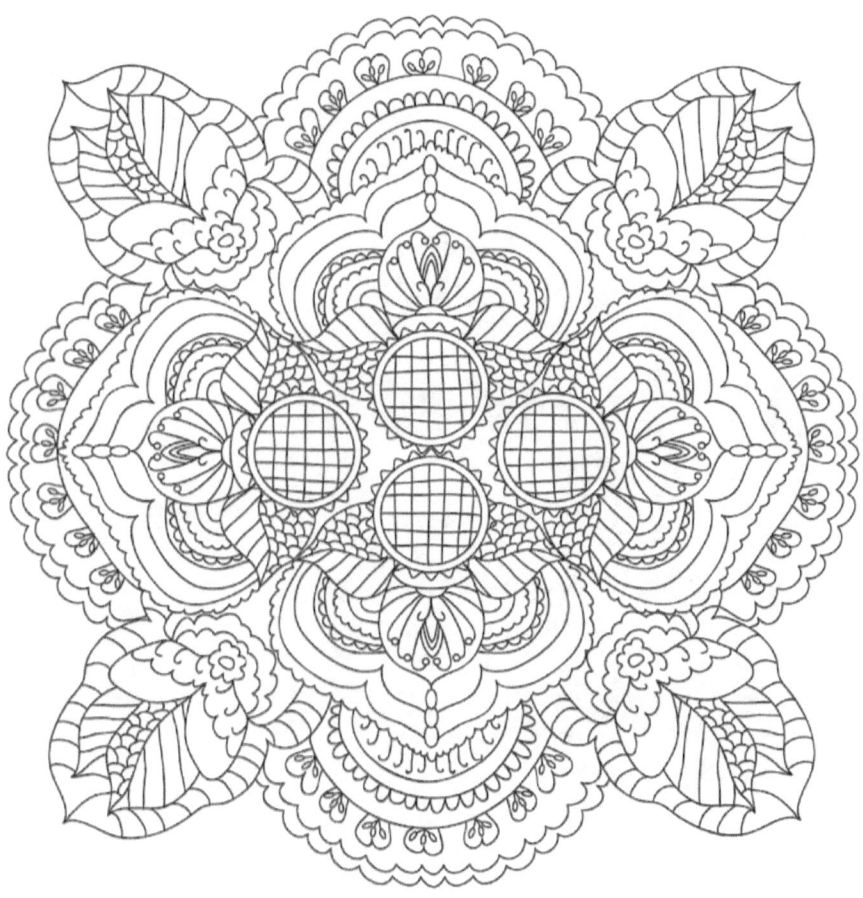

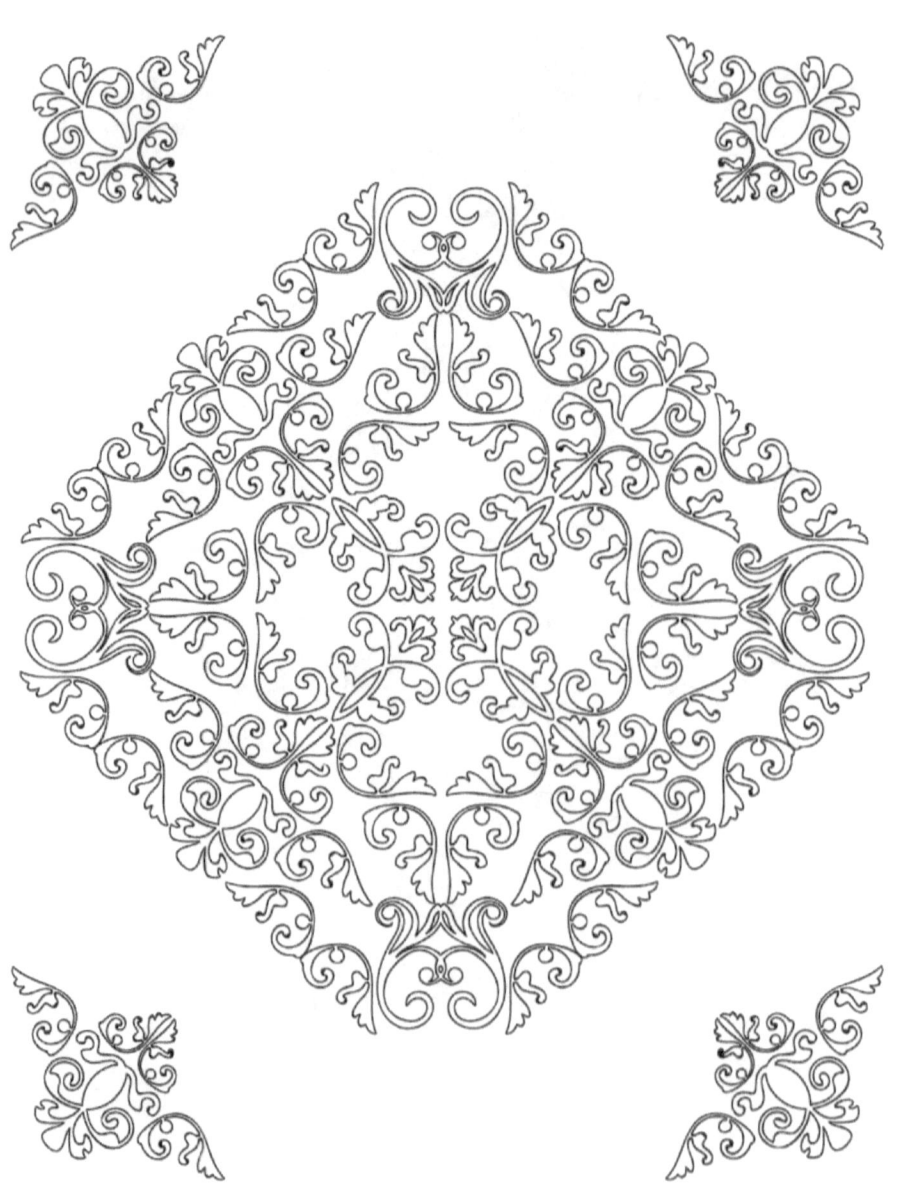

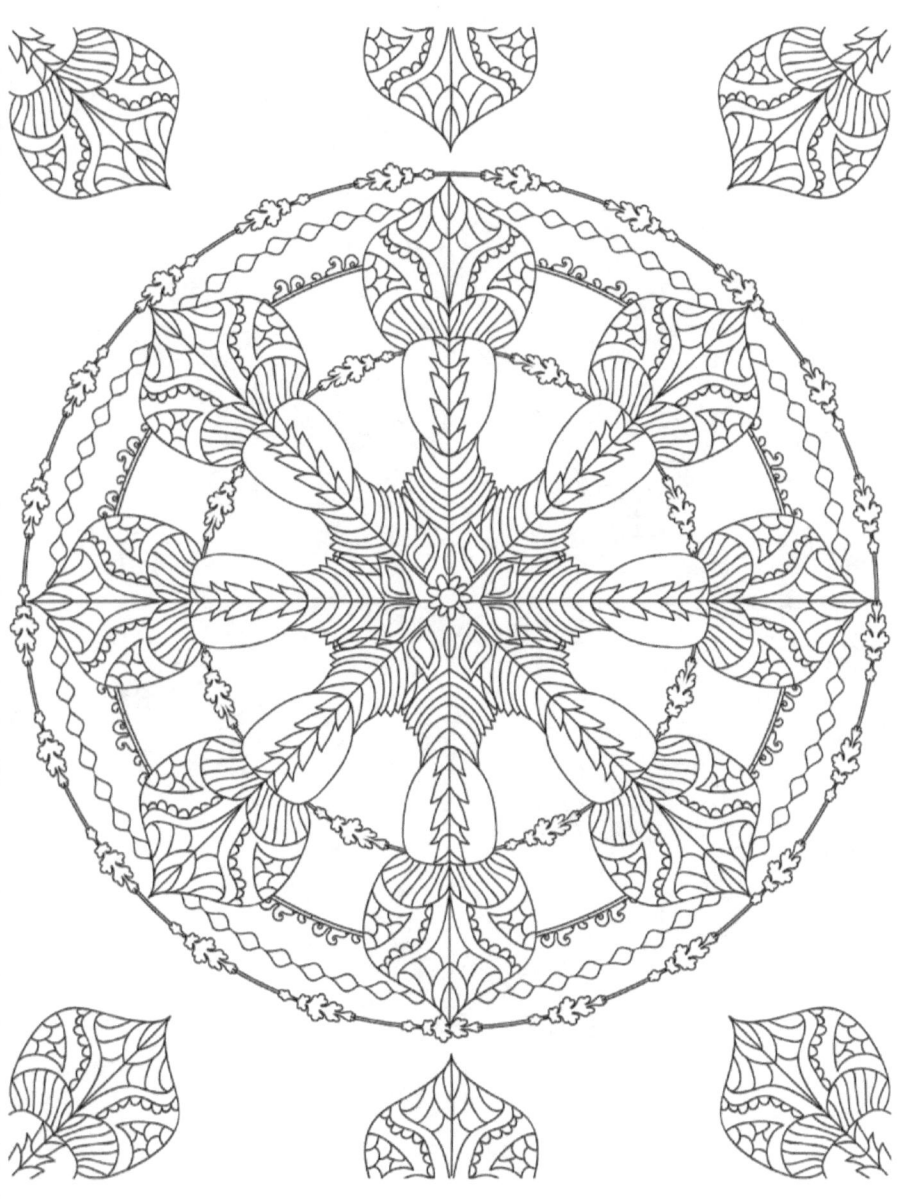

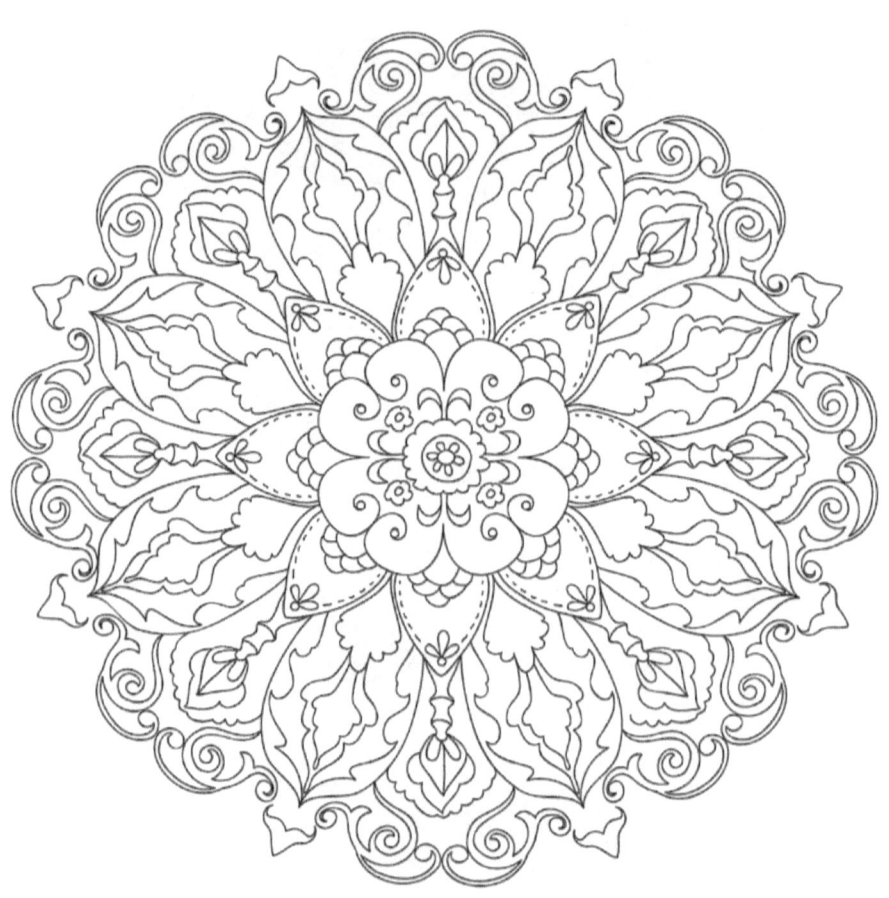

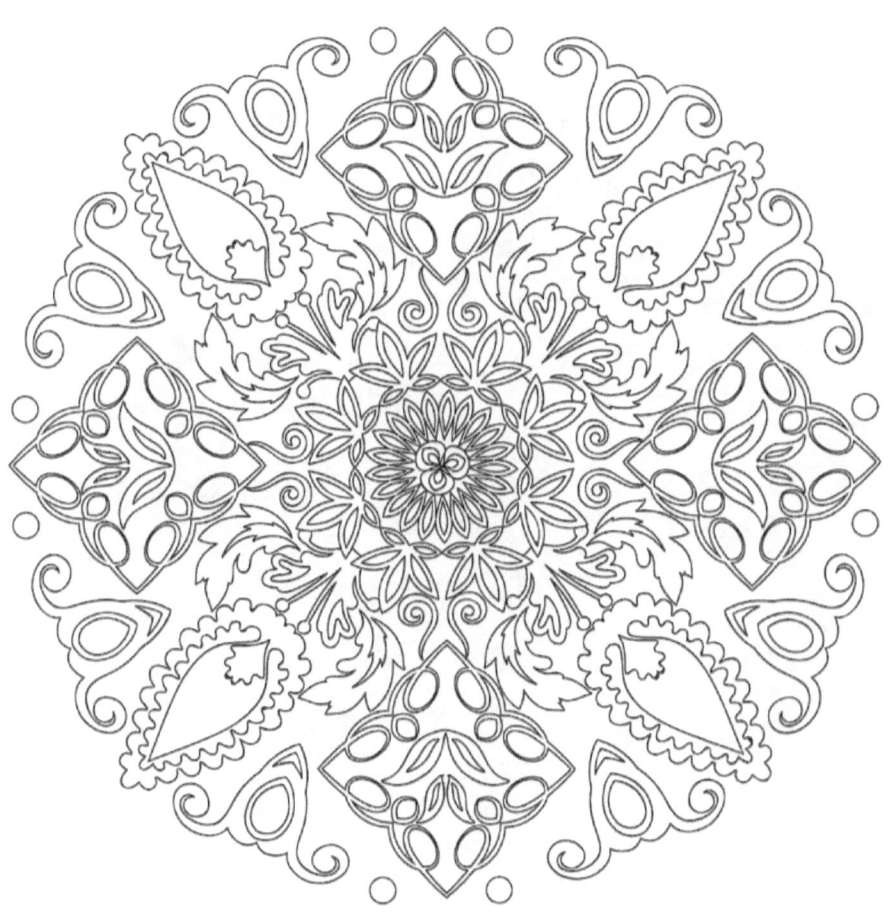

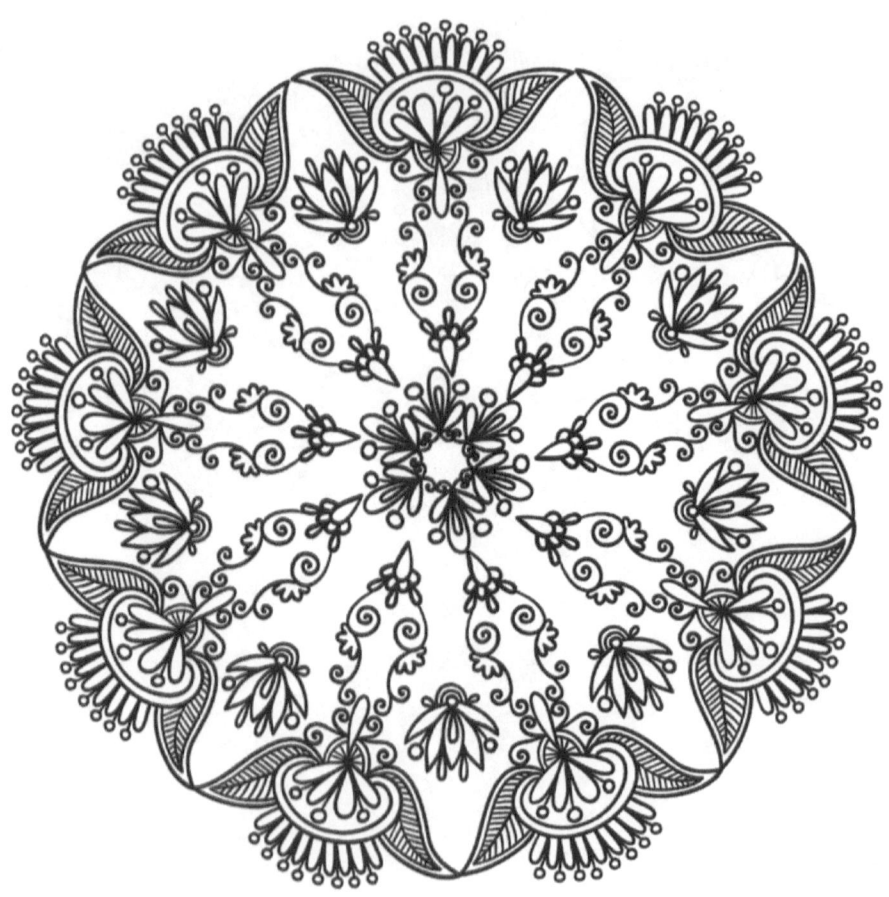

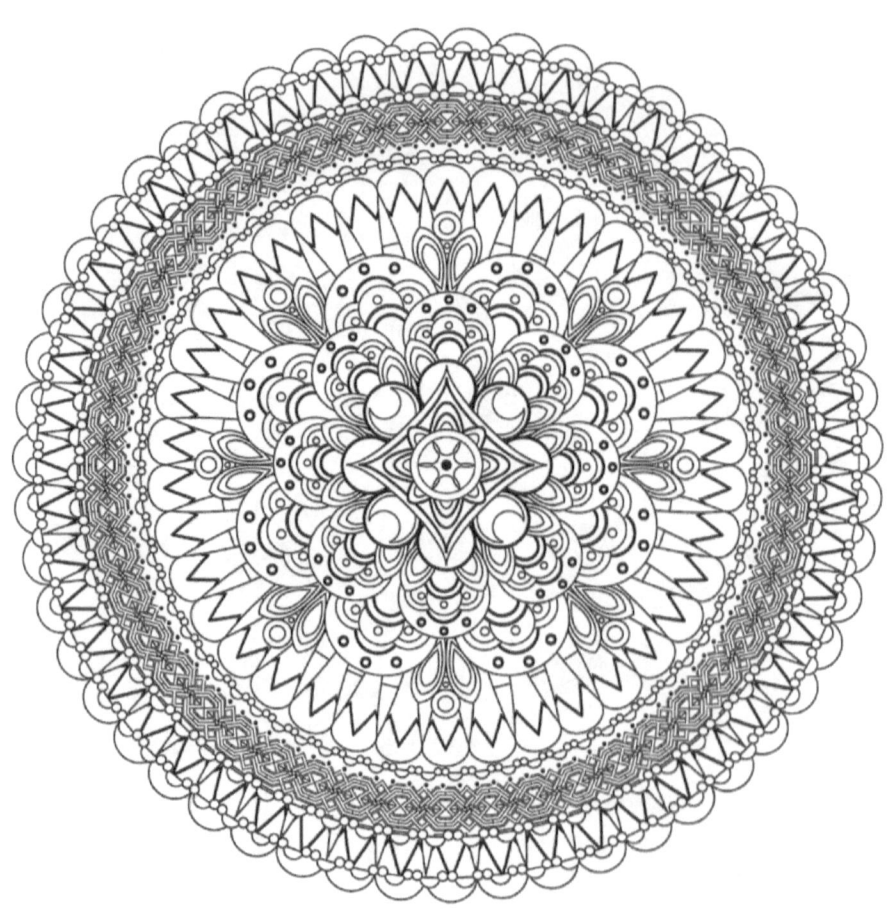

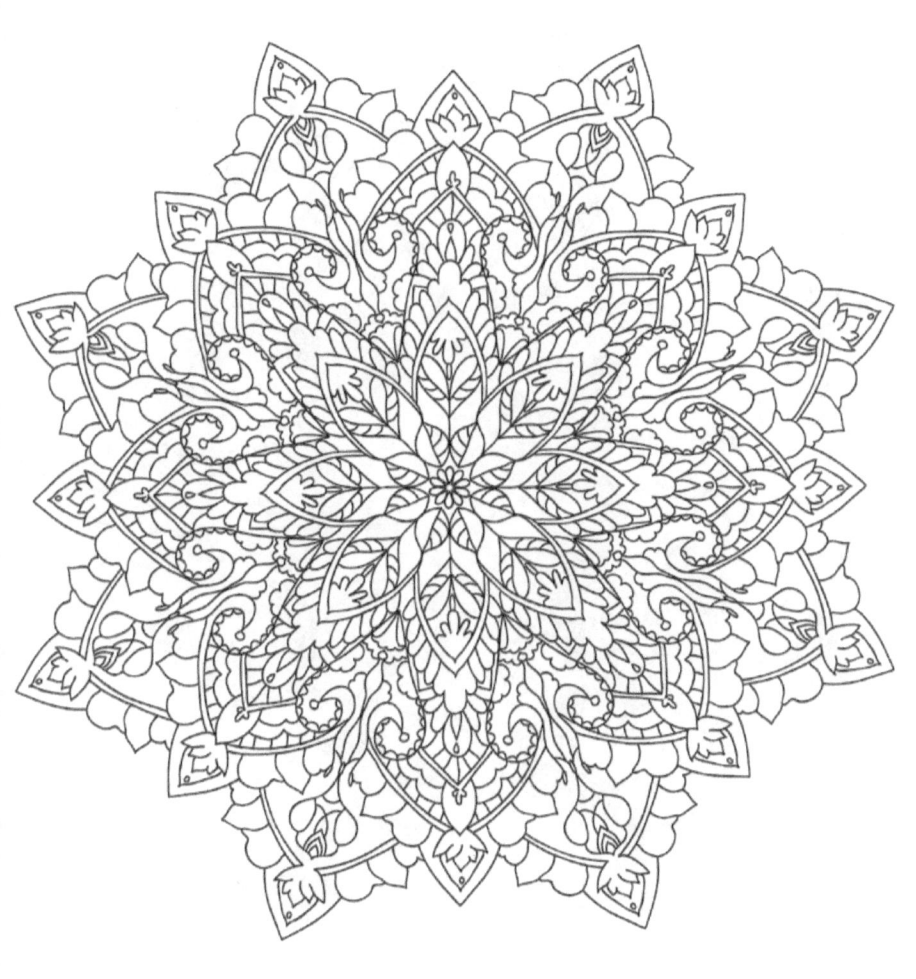

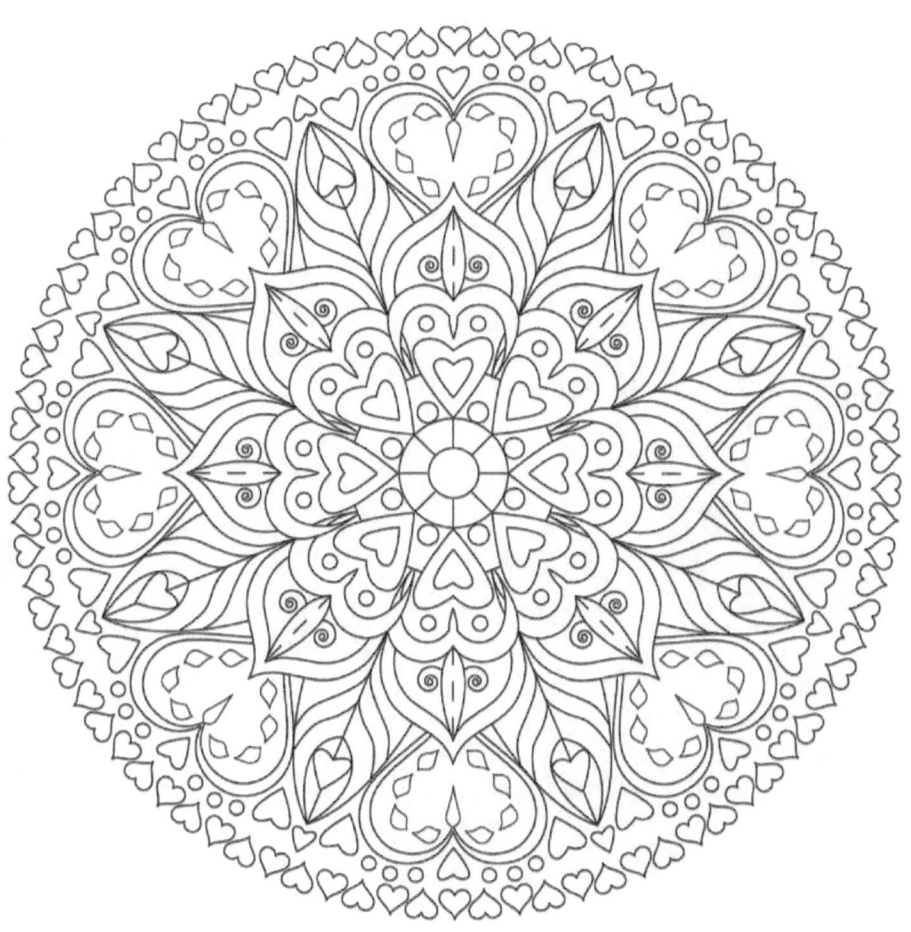

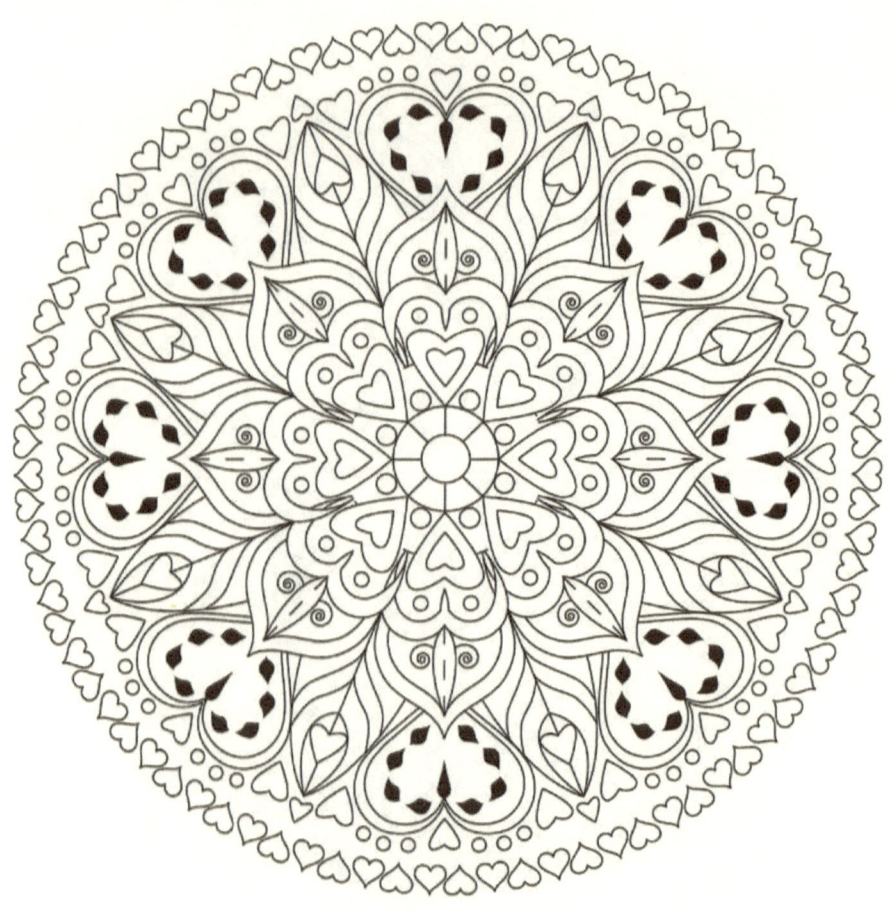

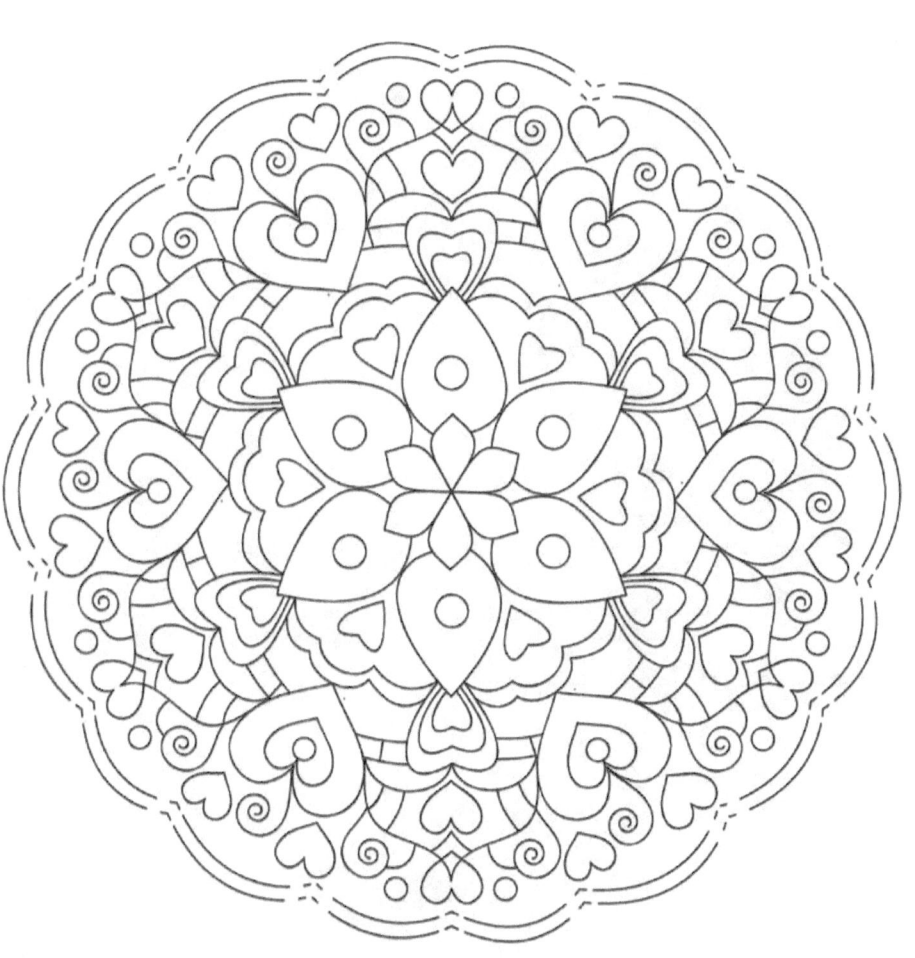

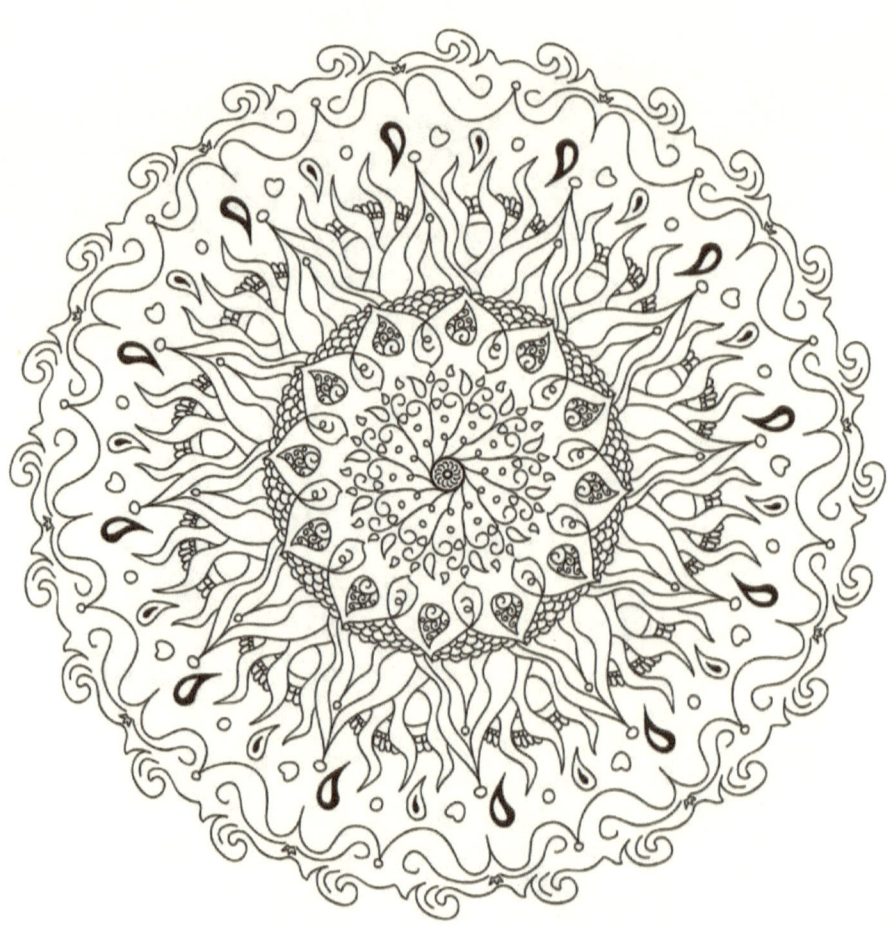

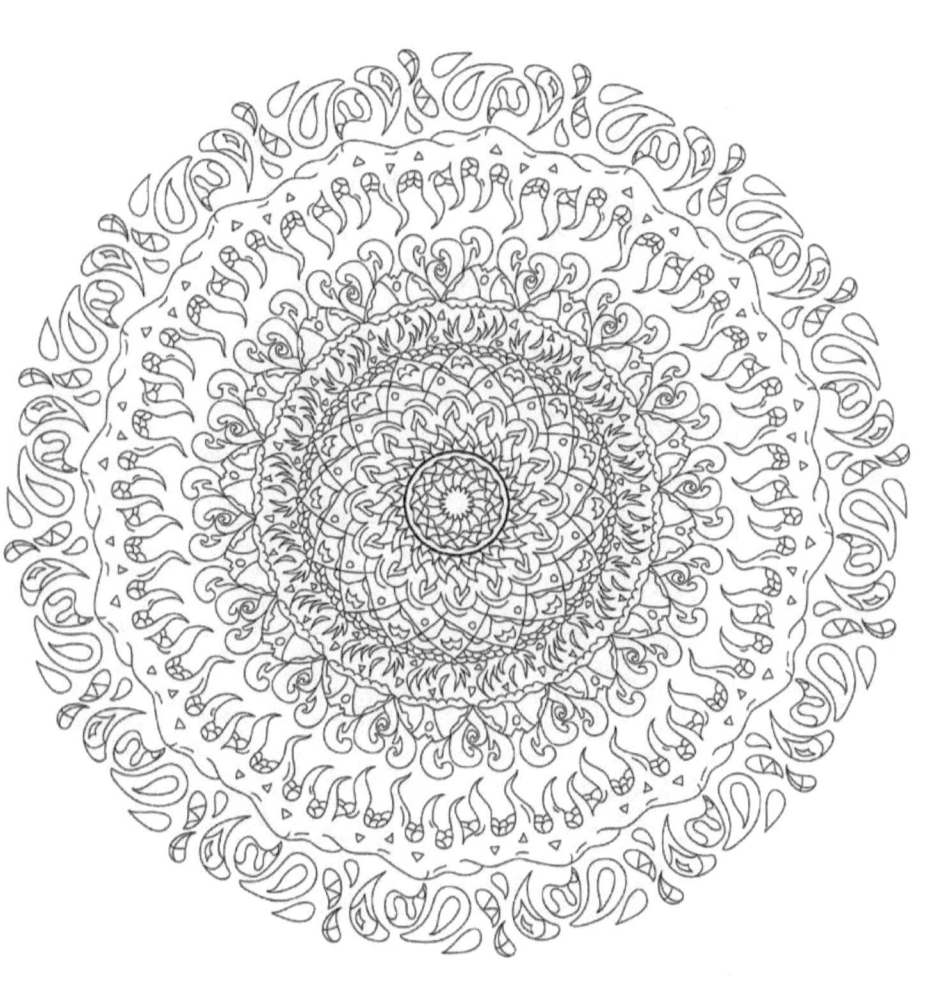

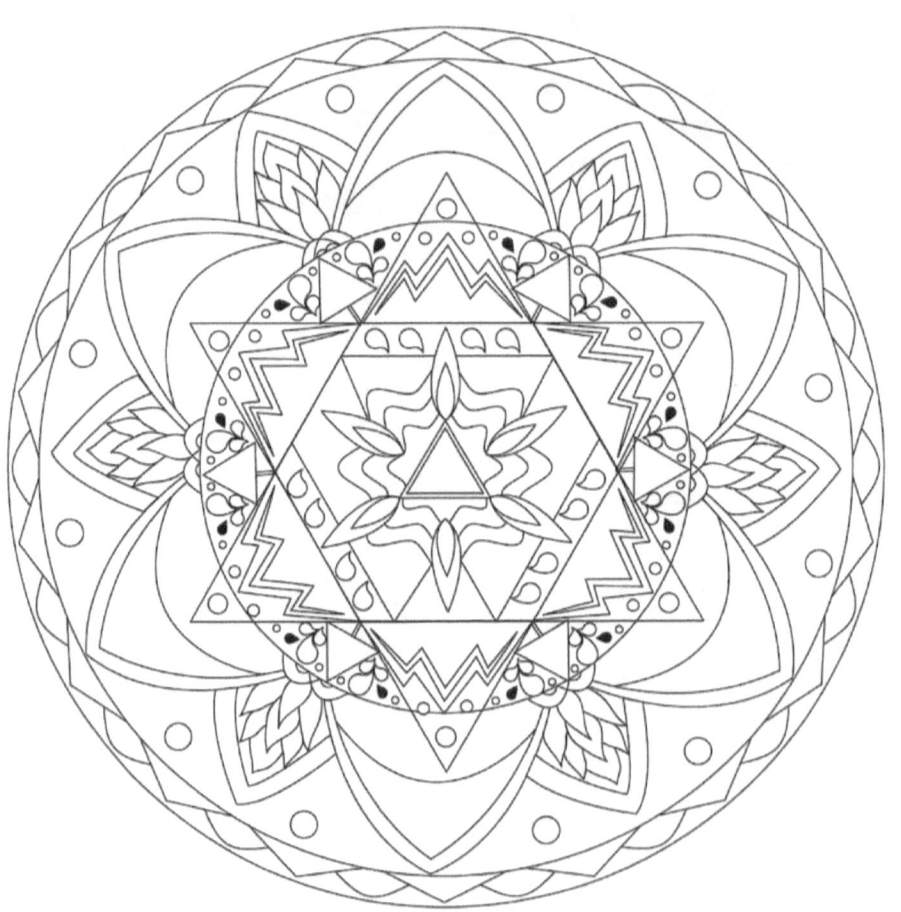

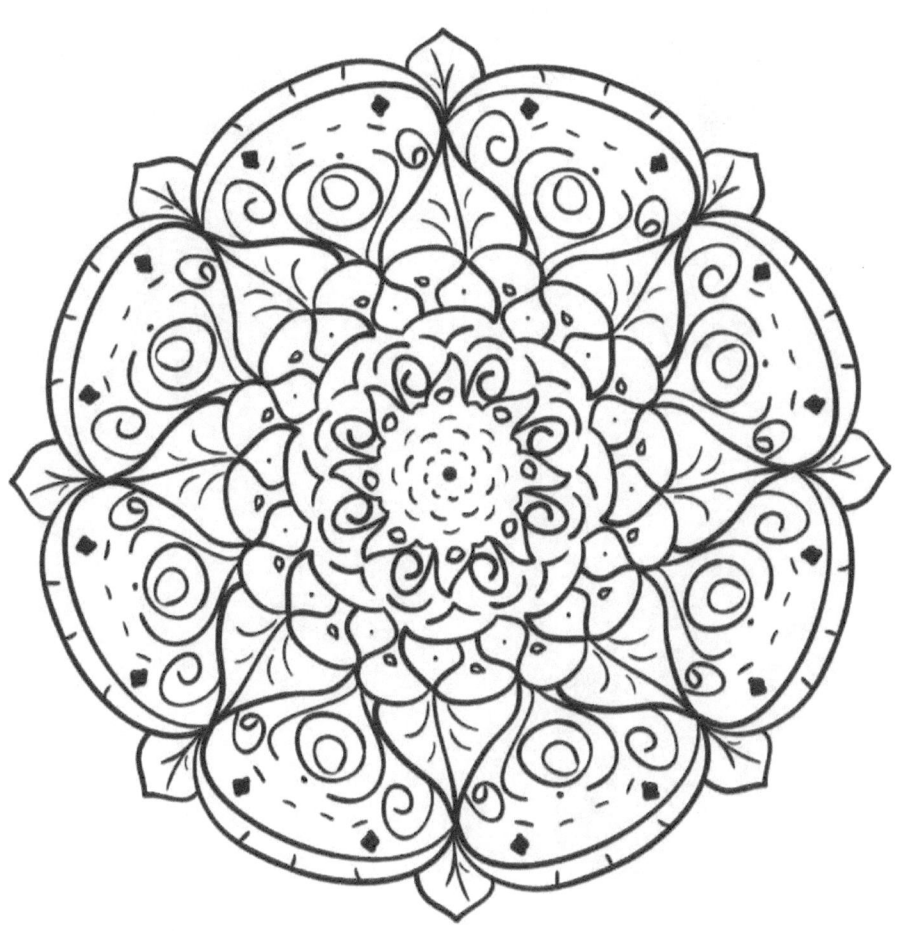

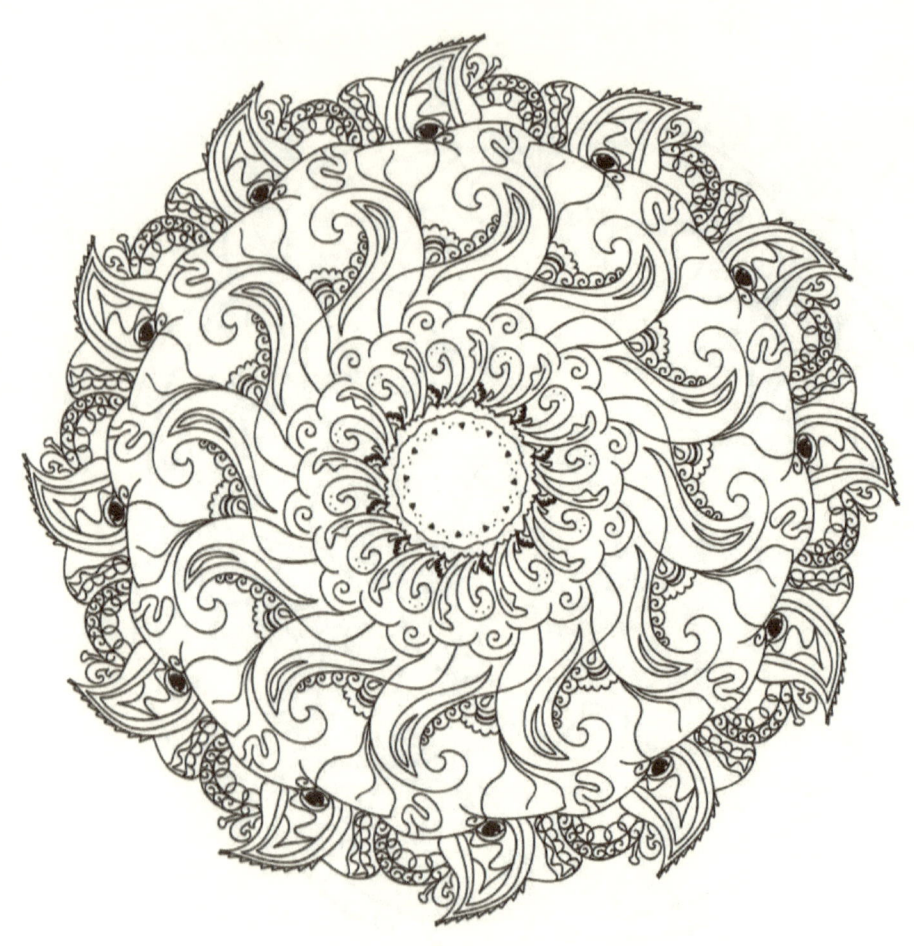

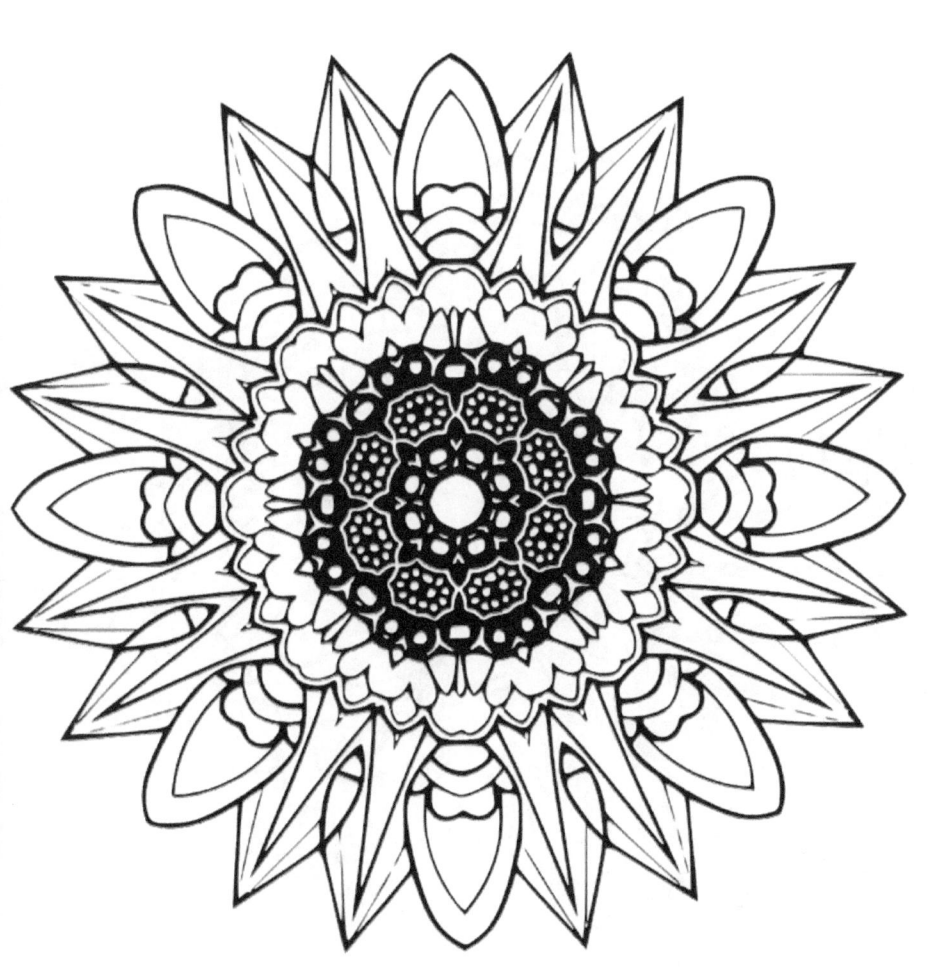

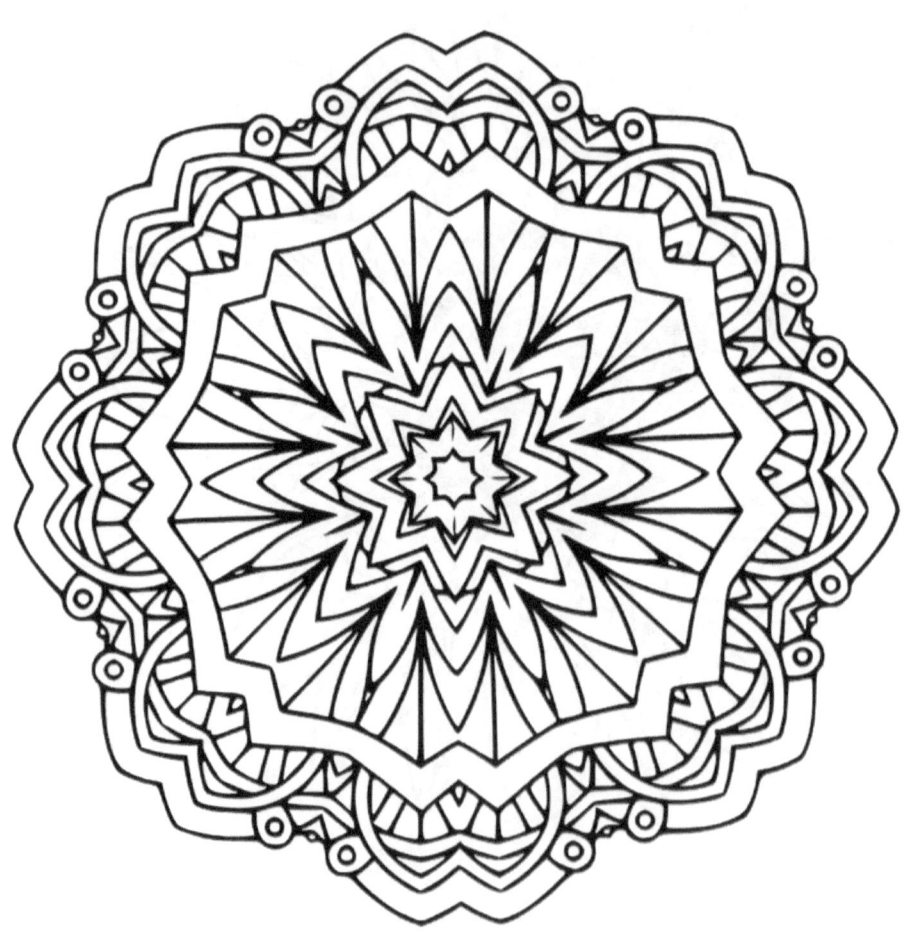

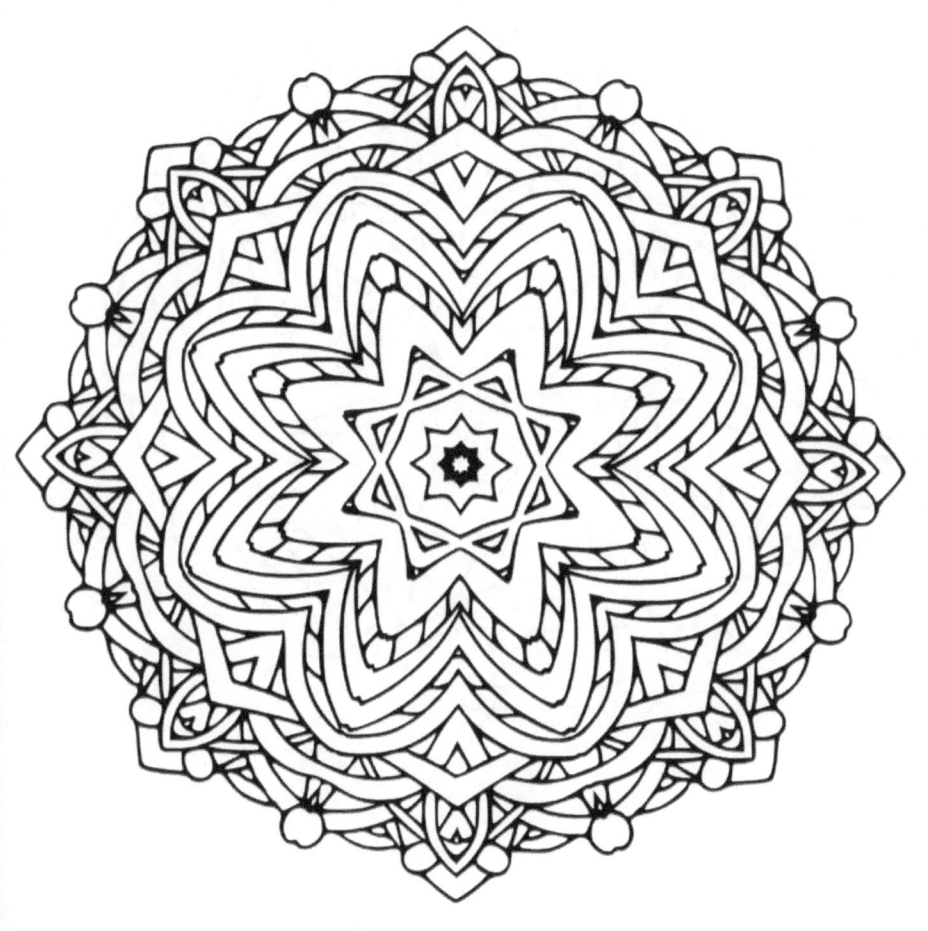

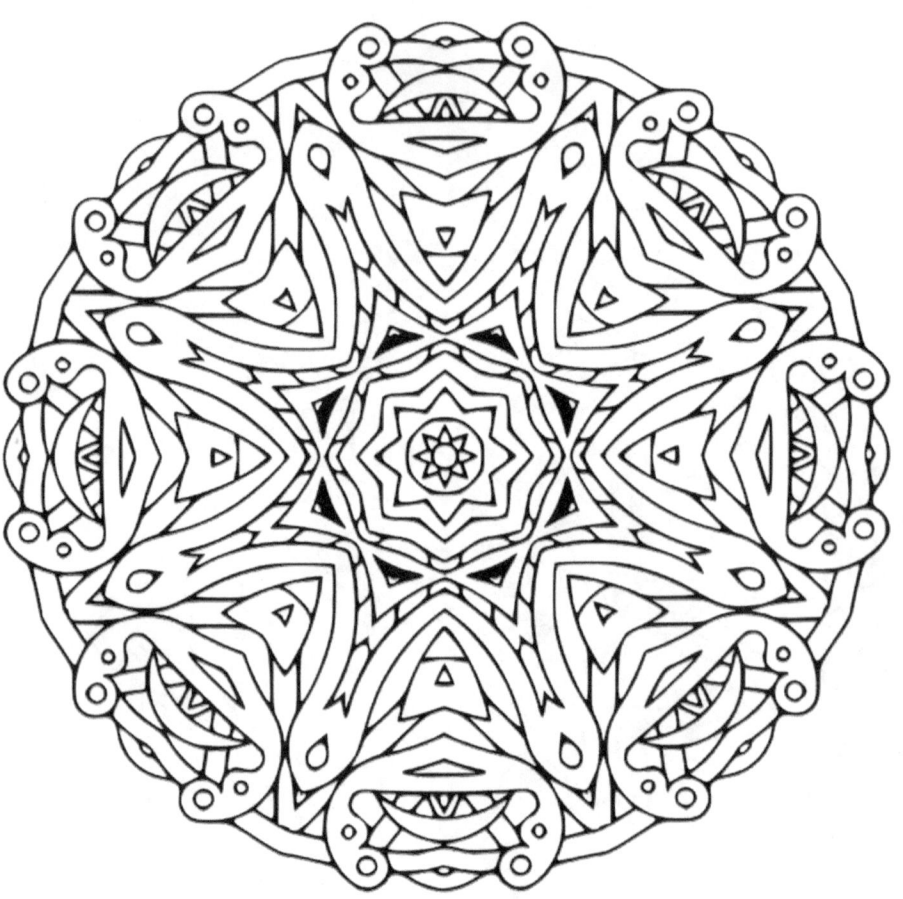

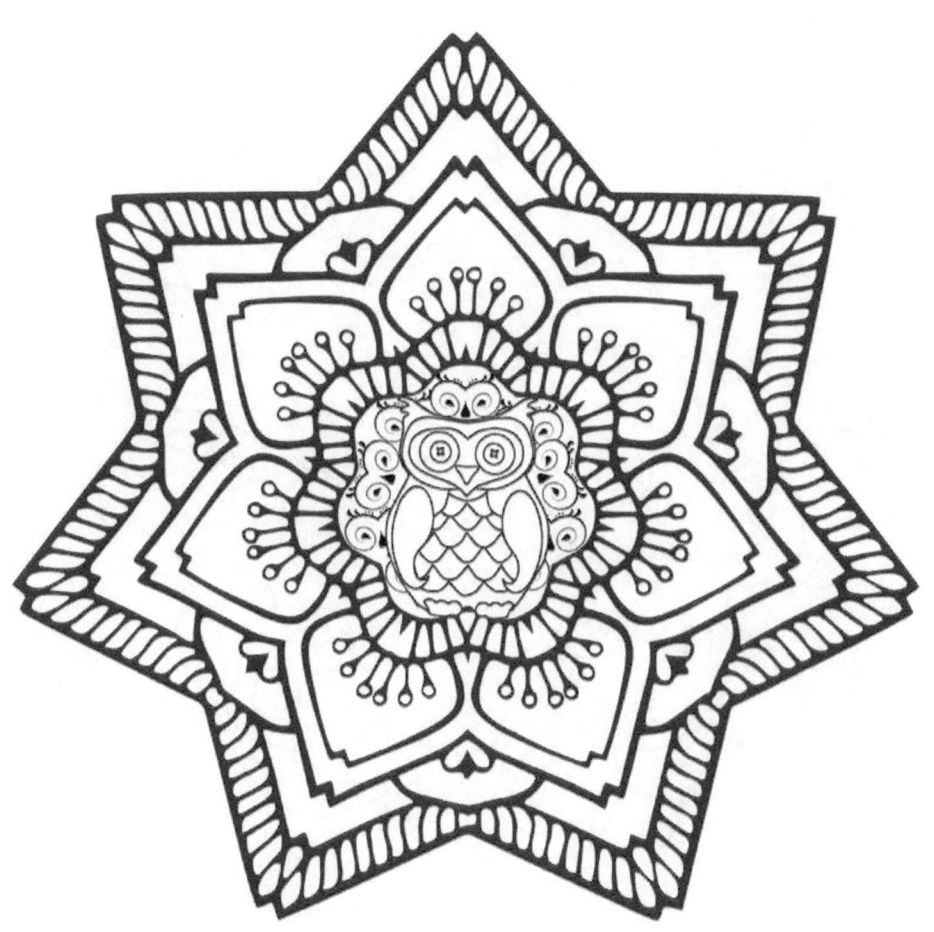

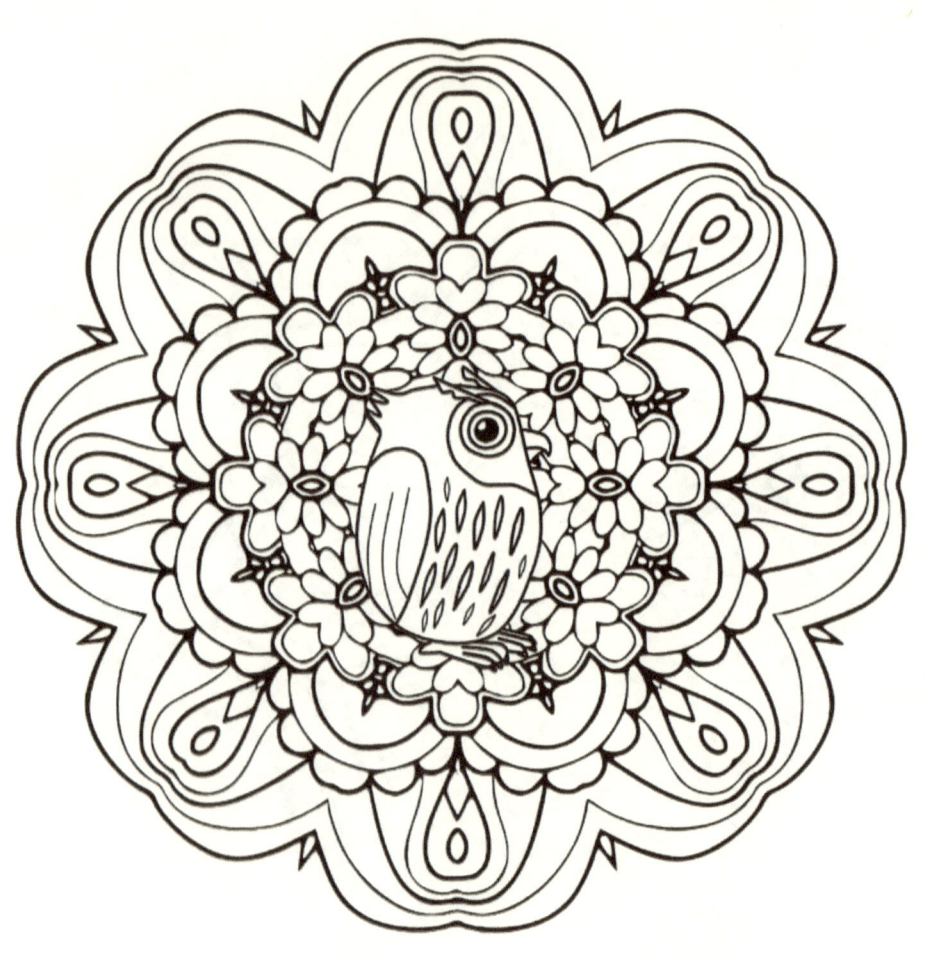

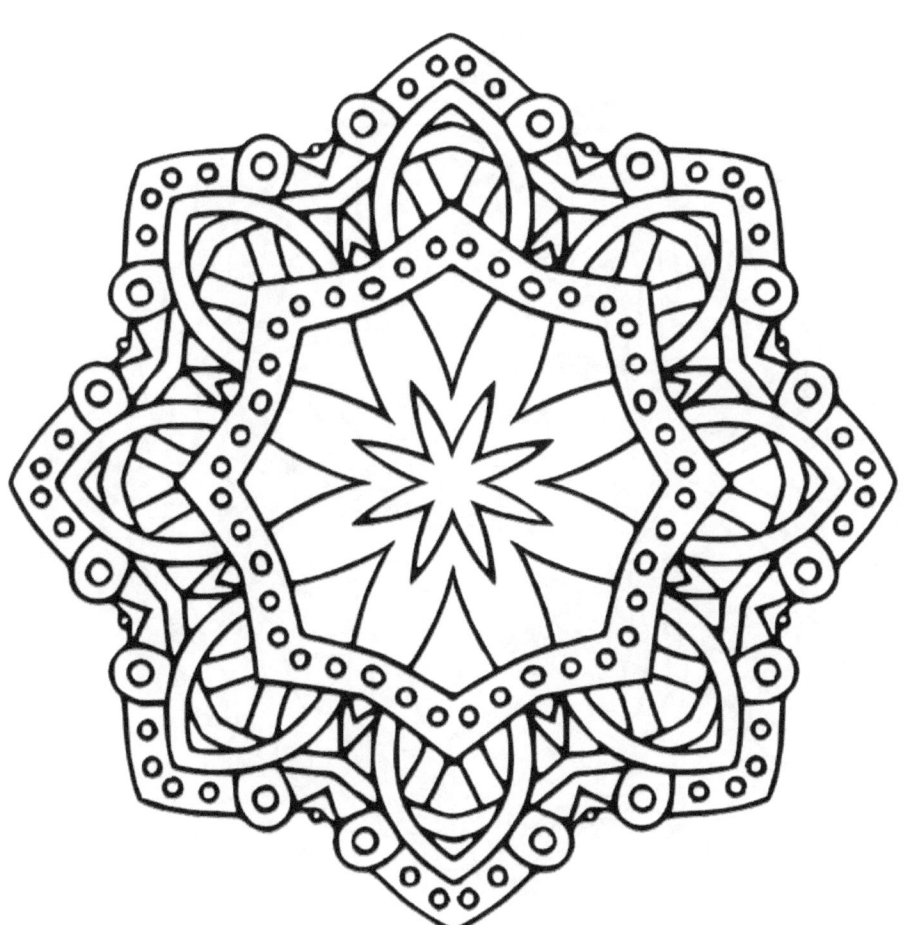

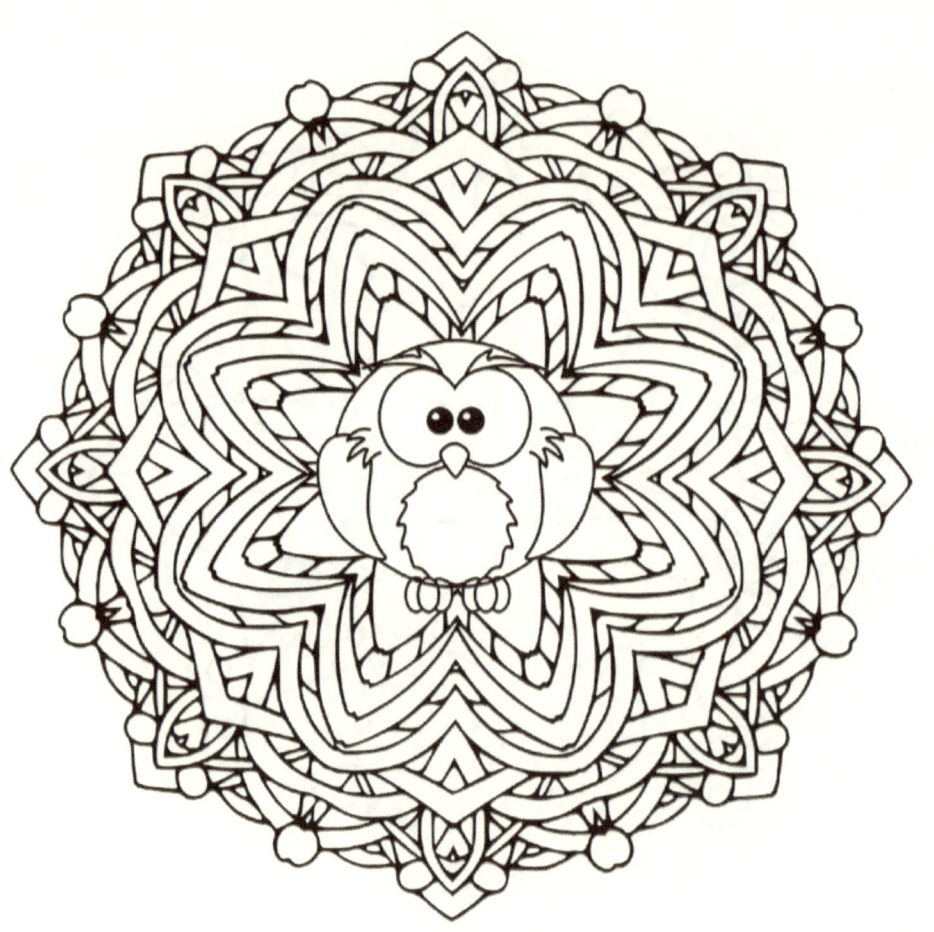

www.ingramcontent.com/pod-product-compliance
Lightning Source LLC
Chambersburg PA
CBHW022132170526
45157CB00004B/1856